Michael Adams
Development of a Grandmaster

PERGAMON CHESS BOOKS

Executive Editor: Paul Lamford
Technical Editor: Jimmy Adams
Russian Series Editor: Kenneth Neat

Some other books in this series:

A full catalogue of Pergamon Chess books is available from:
Pergamon Chess, London Road, Wheatley, Oxford OX9 1YR, U.K.

Michael Adams
Development of a
Grandmaster

by
Bill and Michael Adams

PERGAMON CHESS

Member of Maxwell Macmillan Pergamon Publishing Corporation

OXFORD · NEW YORK · BEIJING · FRANKFURT

SEOUL · SYDNEY · TOKYO

UK	Pergamon Press plc, Headington Hill Hall, Oxford OX3 0BW, England
USA	Pergamon Press Inc, Maxwell House, Fairview Park, Elmsford, New York 10523, USA
PEOPLE'S REPUBLIC OF CHINA	Maxwell Pergamon China, Beijing Exhibition Centre, Xizhimenwai Dajie, Beijing 100044, PRC
GERMANY	Pergamon Press GmbH, Hammerweg 6, D-6242 Kronberg, Federal Republic of Germany
AUSTRALIA	Maxwell Macmillan Pergamon Publishing Australia Pty Ltd, Lakes Business Park, 2 Lord Street, Botany, NSW 2019, Australia
JAPAN	Pergamon Press, 5th Floor, Matsuoka Central Building, 1-7-1 Nishishinjuku, Shinjuku-ku, Tokyo 160, Japan
KOREA	Pergamon Press Korea, KPO Box 315, Seoul 110-603, Korea

First Edition 1991

Library of Congress Cataloging-in-Publication Data
Adams, Bill.
Michael Adams: development of a grandmaster /
by Bill and Michael Adams. — 1st ed.
p. cm. — (Pergamon chess series)
Includes indexes.
1. Adams, Michael. 2. Chess players — England — Biography.
3. Chess — Collections of games.
I. Adams, Michael. II. Title. III. Series.
GV1439.A33A63 1991   794.1'092—dc20   91-13452

British Library Cataloguing in Publication Data
Adams, Bill
Michael Adams: development of a grandmaster. —
(Pergamon chess books)
1. Chess
I. Title II. Adams, Michael
794.1092

ISBN 0-08-037802-1

**Distributed in the United States and Canada
by Macmillan Publishing Company/New York
866 Third Avenue, New York NY 10022. 212-702-2000**

Printed in Great Britain by BPCC Wheatons Ltd, Exeter

Contents

Preface

"You are too young to play chess. Chess is a game for grown-ups. Perhaps when you are eighteen, you might learn to play chess."

I regret that they were hardly encouraging words to greet an enthusiastic youngster, expressing an interest in the game. However they were the words that I used to Michael.

After all, I had reached my mid-thirties, without suffering through its absence among my interests. Vaguely, despite some memories of the publicity surrounding the Fischer-Spassky match, I imagined chess to be a game for pipe smoking gentlemen of retirement age and not the sort of thing for our youngster.

Besides I did not know how to play the game myself. I had been brought up on draughts and my only contact with chess had been when I was given a set of pieces. As I had no contacts with anyone who played the game, the set was put away in a cupboard and forgotten.

My wife, Margaret, and I had returned to our native Cornwall, after teaching in London, to buy our first house and bring up a family. Michael was our first born child and just a year and a half later, Janet was born.

Michael was a child with tremendous energy and stamina. He would walk for miles and miles and still not be tired enough to go to bed at a normal bedtime. There were three main interests in his life, namely soldiers, steam engines and mechanical diggers. I cannot explain this range of interests as none originated from his parents, although I suppose we went along with his enthusiasms. Whenever he was given money to spend, it would be taken down to Mr. and Mrs. Plummer in the Post Office at Perranporth, where we lived, and he would take ages looking at all the toy soldiers, before making his selection.

He showed considerable aptitude for games, generally using soldiers for counters whenever possible and adjusting the rules or the setting to have military significance. He even learned to read by shooting down words and when he went to school, he insisted on calling his first headteacher, "Captain" Delbridge.

One day, I thought that I would introduce him to draughts. He was always enthusiastic about learning a new game, but when I took out the draughts board, he was more excited than usual. However as I opened the tin containing the pieces and began placing them on the board, he complained that I was using the wrong pieces, as he pointed to the pictures of knights, rooks, kings and queens that surrounded the board. I explained that they belong to another game called chess and that was when I made my pronouncement on the game.

My answer did not satisfy Michael and he persisted in his demands to play the game. Looking back, it was almost as if he knew it was a game for him. To increase the pressure on his parents, he began to demand the right to stop in the main street and look at a small wooden chess set in a craft shop window. We should have bought the set for him, I suppose, but I thought that I could be as determined as him. I should have known better.

On one particular occasion, when he was being more stubborn than usual, I suddenly remembered the chess set that I had been given. When we had moved into the house, I had collected a lot of my childhood possessions and put them up in the loft. I remarked to Michael that I thought that I had a chess set in the loft. You should have seen him move. Before long, I was clambering around the loft and searching for the chessmen.

When they were handed to him, he could not have been more pleased. He made up his own games with the pieces for a while, but before long he began to demand to play the real game.

Reluctantly, I decided to do something about it.

1 How the Game Was Learned

I have read several accounts of how various players learned to play chess in amazingly quick time. Michael was definitely not one of them, although how long it did take is not clear. We never realised that countless people were going to ask when he learned to play, as we did not have the remotest idea of how things were going to turn out. All timings are guesswork before the age of eight, but I would guess that he was about six when he first laid his hands on the chess pieces.

Michael always showed an intense interest in everything that appealed to him, but absolute boredom and disinterest in other things, whereas Janet would dabble in most things and then go on to something else. Thus we might spend an hour or so with Michael watching a JCB on a building site or a whole day attending a traction engine rally. They were not things that greatly interested us, but it was no great hardship to be there, especially if you could read a newspaper or a book at the same time. We reckoned that in time, these phases would pass.

To satisfy Michael's demands to play chess, I obtained a book about the game. I cannot recall how it came into my possession or which book it was. As I do not have the book now, I assume that I borrowed the book from the library van, which made weekly visits to Perranporth in those days. I found the book hard going and did not read it all. However I managed to master the instructions on how the board was set up, how the pieces moved and how they captured, thinking that should be enough for any six year old.

Armed with this information, I began to teach the details to Michael. Realising that I only knew some of the rules, I did not give him all the information at once, also thinking that the thrills would last longer that way. I can remember that we started with the pawns and played lots of games with them. Next, I introduced the rooks, as they seemed sensible pieces to me as they always travelled in straight lines and changed directions at right angles. We must have gone on to the other pieces, but my memory of this is not clear. However I can remember playing rook

1

and pawn games with Michael. I can also remember him making up his own games, in which the pieces always moved and captured in the correct way, but with other adaptations of the rules. There was never any castling, checking or mating, as these aspects of the game were in chapters that I had either not read or not understood. Certainly I did not take the library book out again, partly because I did not particularly want to and partly because Michael was perfectly happy, with the limited information that he had. I suppose that he might have even thought that was all there was to chess. If ever I was unavailable to play and Michael wanted someone to play with, then Margaret had to play. Unlike myself, she does not like or understand many games, but Michael would write the moves down for her and using her "notes" she would play games with him.

I played a full game of chess before Michael. News of the interest in chess at the Adams household must have spread and a friend and neighbour, Richard Howell, invited me to have a game one evening. As I had always enjoyed a fair success rate at draughts, I went along, dreaming of exhibiting my new skills. Richard was very thoughtful about his play, but my efforts were rather primitive, with opening moves like 1 h4 2 ♖h3 and 3 ♖e3, as I had spent so long playing rook and pawn games. When he castled, it seemed rather unfair as I had spent my time lining the rook up with his king, only for him to play a move that I did not know anything about, so rather sheepishly I asked him for an explanation and he told me all about castling. As the game developed, so I learned other things, which I was able to pass on to Michael the next day.

I am not sure how long it was afterwards that Michael played his first full game. It may have been with me, but if it was, I have forgotten about it. However I do remember visiting good friends, Ray and Maureen Woodhouse, and when we arrived, Ray was playing chess with their children, who are a couple of years older than ours. When Ray began to pack the game away, I intervened and told them how interested Michael was in chess, so they carried on playing, while we went off to the lounge. In a short while, we were joined by their children, who explained that Michael and Ray were still playing. I am not sure how long it was before they rejoined us, but I do remember their expressions. Poor Ray was looking slightly embarrassed as he tried to console a very tearful Michael, who had lost a game, and to explain how well he thought Michael had played. Michael was not at all interested in this praise. He had always hated losing, whatever the game was, and it was just the same with chess.

We certainly had lots of games of chess together. I believe that Michael won most of them. If he did win a game, I would hurriedly set the board up again, thinking my luck would change soon, but it rarely did. However on the few occasions that Michael lost, he would refuse to play any more that evening.

In the summer of 1978, we moved to Falmouth to live, as I had been appointed headteacher of King Charles Junior School in the previous Autumn. Michael's interest in chess deepened about this time. One of the factors was the fact that the school had a chess club, run by Ray Rice and Harry Trumbell, two hard working teachers. Initially I had not taken much interest in the club, other than making it clear that I was aware of its existence and of the hard work put in by the two teachers. However during the new school year beginning in September 1978, I found myself being increasingly drawn to the lunchtime sessions and watching with interest. I also encouraged the teachers to arrange matches against other schools. This was rather unfair as Harry and Ray were already heavily committed with outdoor sports in the after school sessions. Consequently I became more involved with the chess club.

At the end of each day, Michael wanted to know what had happened at chess club and whether there was anything to pass on to him. Thus he learned details such as the en passant rule, different ways that draws could be obtained and knowledge of some basic openings.

Another factor was that Falmouth had a permanent library and Michael had found some more chess books. We discovered that you had to learn descriptive notation before many of these books became understandable and when we had done this, we were able to dip into "Modern Chess Openings" and look up details of some of his favourite openings, which included the King's Gambit and the Sicilian Najdorf.

Michael's first real test in chess came at one of the King Charles' early matches. He was still only at Infants' School, but his mum brought him along to one of our matches against All Saints, another local school, so that he could see what went on. When one of our top boards lost quickly, I asked Michael Sadka, their teacher if Michael could play a friendly against the winner. I was quite amazed, as well as relieved, to see that not only did Michael hold his own against a boy five years older than himself but he defeated him. I put it down to beginner's luck, instead of getting excited about it. One of my regrets is that Michael never played competitive chess at an earlier age. I am not thinking that it hampered his progress, merely that he was prevented from having lots of enjoyment, which the games would undoubtedly have brought him.

My next task was to go along to the local Chess Club, which met at a local social club, according to the information displayed at the library. By this time, it was the summer of 1979 and I discovered that some chess clubs do not meet in the summer months and Falmouth Chess Club was one of them. However I was fortunate that the secretary was at the club and I was able to ask for details, not mentioning that I was enquiring for my seven year old son until near the end. I was relieved to hear that he would be welcomed, provided that he could play chess, behave himself and be accompanied by an adult, all of which suited us fine.

2   Early Competitions

In the Autumn of 1979, Michael joined King Charles Junior School. To say that he had been looking forward to that time would be something of an understatement, although it had nothing to do with Mathematics or English or any other classroom subject. For Michael, it simply meant that school would become a more attractive place as there was a chance of playing chess there.

As fortune would have it, my own involvement with the chess scene had increased to the extent that I had found out what was happening in Cornwall Junior Chess. The annual Primary Schools Congress was to be held on November 17th, which just happened to be Michael's eighth birthday. I decided that the Congress was going to be the focal point of school chess activity. Therefore I added two extra chess sessions, which took place after school, and selected a group of about twenty children, who seemed to get the best results. The children covered a considerable age span and in fact there were very few fourth year juniors, while there was one other first year junior besides Michael. I was pleased about this, as I reckoned that it would be quite a long programme before we became as good as some of the other schools that I had heard about.

The main aim of my initial chess sessions was to increase the competitiveness of the children. I hoped that this would make them determined to play up to their ability level and that it would reduce the number of silly mistakes that they made. However I did have another motive and that was that I realised that I was ill equipped to be teaching chess to them. By organising mini leagues, I provided the competitive aspect that they enjoyed and also concealed my own deficiencies. However I soon became dissatisfied with what was happening, as the end of the session would often come just when the game was getting interesting and it seemed as if a lot of effort had achieved little. By teaching the rest of the children to record their games and then insisting that they did so, it meant that the game could be continued at a later time. Another thing that I did was to start their games from an interesting point

5

that had either occurred in one of their games or else one that I had found in a newspaper or book. Then I would make them play from that point with both black and white against different opponents, recording their moves as they did so. Towards the end of the session, I would gather the children together and either show them the line played in the book or paper or else lead a discussion as to which plans had been most successful in continuing their games.

Michael performed quite well in these situations and was certainly among the best players in the group, although it was not uncommon to see him come off second best.

Partly with the congress in mind and partly because I thought it would give him considerable pleasure, I took Michael along to Falmouth Chess Club. About ten adults gathered there most Tuesday evenings. Most seemed to have their regular playing partners, with whom they would quite happily settle down to an evening's chess. However I soon discovered that if I asked, they were quite happy to play against Michael, although it would not have occurred to them to ask him for a game, presumably because they thought it unlikely that a seven year old would give them a good evening's chess. Initially I was asked to play more often than Michael and I would transfer the invitation to him, if he was not playing. Otherwise I would decline politely, being petrified of making a fool of myself.

There were two members of about BCF, that is British Chess Federation, 150 strength, which indicated that they were quite strong club players. Indeed one of them, Philip Breach, was an ex-county champion. Both of these players seemed particularly keen to play Michael and Philip always made a point of discussing the game with Michael afterwards. It was interesting to watch Michael at these post mortems. He never said very much, but showed that he was contributing by quietly gliding pieces around the board.

Eventually the big day came – Michael's birthday and his first chess congress. I decided to take about a dozen of the children, who were obtaining the best results, to Truro for the event. We did not quite know what to expect and were quite surprised to find over one hundred in Michael's event, the Cornwall Under 10 championship. There were nearly as many as in the Under 11 event as well. Our children were quite amazed to see row upon row of chess boards, with sets containing pawns that were as big as the kings in our school sets.

It was noticeable that some of our children relished the situation, while others were quite overwhelmed by it all. I could not quite decide which category Michael came into. He never said very much, but then he rarely did. The first six rounds were pre-drawn, presumably because of the big numbers. I imagine the draw was done on a random basis and it did not signify very much to me, when Michael won his first six games, as it could have been that all his opponents were weak players.

When the final four rounds were reached, the draw was made on Swiss lines with each player paired with someone doing as well or as badly as themselves. I realised that the big test would be when Michael started playing other players, who had won all of their games as well. However he did not seem to find it a lot harder, although he did stalemate with a proliferation of queens in one round.

Eventually the last round was reached and Michael shared the lead with a lad called Jon Prunty from the host school, with eight and a half points each from their nine games. Their game was hard fought and was still undecided at the end of the stipulated time. To ensure that the prizegiving was not held up, a chess clock was introduced and both players were allowed five minutes each for the remainder of their moves. I remember thinking how unfair this was, especially as I had been trying to get Michael to play slower all day. Now, all of a sudden, he had to speed up, using a device that he had never used previously. I need not have worried. Michael took it all in his stride and won very quickly, once the clock was introduced, to win his first chess championship. Another King Charles boy, Jeremy Varney, finished second to Michael, so we felt that it had been a reasonable day.

The next chess landmark came nearly three weeks later, when Falmouth Chess Club found themselves short of a player, just before they were due to travel to St. Ives for a league fixture. The club secretary lived near us and he called at the house and asked if Michael would be able to play, making it clear that he would have little chance of winning, but it would be better than defaulting on one board. After I had found out a little more about the match, I said that Michael could play, as long as I travelled with him. As there were no other alternatives, I did get my way.

I know that Michael was pleased that I did travel with him that evening and on every other chess occasion in the first few years of his chess career. Perhaps there are eight, nine and ten year olds, who can cope on their own, but Michael was certainly not one of them. In any case, it is my experience that other chess playing adults are blissfully unaware of children's needs, assuming that if they can play chess, then they can sort out everything else. Thus children might be expected to know the time controls without being told, find the toilets in a strange building, drink strong tea and coffee, put up with cigarette smoke and countless other things that a regular adult member of the side would take for granted. My policy was always to be near the playing area, where Michael could easily find me if he needed to, but not to be hovering near his board.

Anyway, despite the secretary's forebodings, Michael did win his game, helping Falmouth to win the match by four points to two. As it was his first recorded game, it is given below. All of the comments on the games in this book are by the 1990 Michael, who finds it difficult to accept that he played some of these moves!

Game 1   7.12.79
P.Land-Adams
Cornish League
St Ives v. Falmouth, Board Six
English Opening

1	c4	e5
2	♘c3	♘f6
3	d3	♗c5
4	e4	d6
5	♗e2	♘c6
6	a3	♗d7
7	♗g5	h6
8	♗xf6	♕xf6
9	f3	0-0
10	♘d5	♕d8
11	b4	♗d4
12	♖b1	♗xg1

12 ... a5 or ... f5 would be more accurate, instead of giving up a good bishop. This begins a spell of aimless play by Black.

13	♖xg1	♖e8
14	g3	a6

15	♖f1	♗h3
16	♖g1	b5
17	g4	♕h4+
18	♔d2	♕g5+
19	♔e1	♕h4+
20	♔d2	♕f2

I played 20 ... ♕f2, because of the attraction of White's exposed king. Undoubtedly, there are practical chances for Black to win at this level, but clearly I should have settled for a draw.

21	♕e1	♕xe1+
22	♔xe1	♖a7
23	♖g3	♗xg4
24	♖xg4	♘d4
25	♖b2	

My opponent failed to spot that 25 ♘f6+ would have won immediately.

25	...	♖e6
26	f4	exf4
27	♘xf4	♖e8

28	♔d2	bxc4
29	dxc4	♘xe2

29 ... ♖xe4!.

30	♘xe2	a5
31	c5	♖d8
32	cxd6	♖xd6+
33	♔e3	a4
34	e5	♖e6
35	♖e4	f5
36	♖c4	

36 exf6 e.p. is better. Perhaps we were not absolutely sure of the rule!

36	...	♖xe5+
37	♔f4	♖b5
38	♘d4	♖d5
39	♘xf5	♖d8
40	♖bc2	♖d7
41	b5	♖f7
42	♔e4	♖b7
43	♖xa4	♖xb5
44	♖a7	

White has let me off the hook several times and encouraged my resistance. Now he blunders so badly that he loses all his advantage.

44	...	♖bxf5
45	a4	♖f4+
46	♔d5	

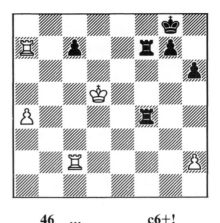

| 46 | ... | c6+! |

The winning of Black's rook by discovered check completes the transformation.

47	♔xc6	♖xa7
48	♔b5	♖axa4
49	♖c8+	♔h7
50	♖c7	♖fb4+
51	♔c6	♖c4+
52	♔d7	♖xc7+
53	♔xc7	♖a2
54	h3	

White **resigned** at this point. Bearing in mind my age, I feel that I played reasonably well at the start and finish of the game, but would describe the middle as pretty mediocre.

Michael did not retain his place for the next match, but he was selected just over a month later, when he defeated Marcus Pilling (BCF 125), who was the strongest of the four league opponents that he played in his first season. He maintained a hundred per cent record for those games.

Game 2   15.1.80
Adams-M.Pilling (BCF 125)
Cornish League
Falmouth v. Newquay, Board Six
King's Indian Defence

1   c4

This is not a case of copying my previous opponent's opening. I played the English Opening regularly throughout my first season, although before that I had played the King's Gambit.

1	...	♘f6
2	♘c3	g6
3	d4	d6
4	♗g5	♗g7
5	♘f3	♘bd7
6	g3	b6
7	♗g2	♗b7
8	0-0	0-0
9	♖e1	h6
10	♗d2	♖b8
11	♕c1	♔h7
12	♖b1	♘g8
13	e3	

Neither side has an understanding of the complexities of a closed King's Indian type position and are manoeuvring hopefully but without any real clear plan.

13	...	e5
14	d5	♘c5
15	♕c2	♗c8
16	b4	♘b7
17	e4	f5
18	♖b2	fxe4

19	♘xe4	♗f5
20	♗c3	♕d7
21	a4	

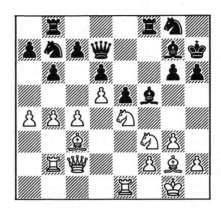

21   ...   ♗h3?

This loses the queen to a simple but effective combination.

22	♗xh3	♕xh3
23	♘3g5+	hxg5
24	♘xg5+	♔h8
25	♘xh3	♘e7
26	♘g5	♖f5
27	♘e6	♘d8
28	♘xc7	

Displaying the greed of an inexperienced player. Of course 28 ♘xg7 is better.

28	...	♖c8
29	♘b5	♘f7
30	♘xa7	♖xc4
31	♖d1	♔h7
32	♖b3	e4
33	♘b5	♘xd5
34	♖c1	♖f3

35	♕b2	♘xc3
36	♘xc3	♘e5
37	♘e2	♘d3
38	♕xg7+!	

I made heavy weather of what should have been a simple technical procedure. Now at last, I get on the right track by simplification.

38	...	♔xg7
39	♖xc4	♖xf2
40	♖xd3	exd3
41	♔xf2	dxe2
42	♔xe2	♔f6
43	♖c6	♔e5
44	♖xb6	d5
45	♖xg6	♔e4
46	a5	**Resigns**

In February, Michael crossed the river Tamar for the first time in his chess career. Ken Butt organised a lot of junior chess in Plymouth over the next few years and I believe this was the first of these occasions. There was an attractive prize list and juniors from all over the south of England entered the tournament. Michael entered the Under 14 section, which included a strong contingent of London Juniors like Michael Hennigan (6½/9) and Aaron Summerscale (6/9). The winner was C.Jenks (7½/9), while Michael's highest placed opponent was John Carlin (7/9), who showed Michael a thing or two in this game.

Game 3   16.2.80
J.Carlin-Adams
Plymouth Under 14 Quickplay
Round Three
Sicilian Defence

1	e4	c5
2	♘f3	d6
3	d4	cxd4
4	♘xd4	♘f6
5	♘c3	g6

At this time my main defence against 1 e4 was the Sicilian Dragon.

6	♗e3	♗g7
7	♕d2	♘g4

8	f3	♘xe3
9	♕xe3	♕b6
10	0-0-0	e5!?

This is a razor sharp continuation that can only be justified by accurate play. A less ambitious and more sensible move was 10 ... ♘c6, especially in view of my limited experience.

11 ♘a4

(see diagram)

11 ...   ♕b4?

11 ... exd4 12 ♘xb6 dxe3 13 ♘xa8 is a better continuation for

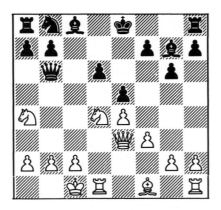

Black, as the pair of bishops and White's out-of-play knight are considerable compensation for being the exchange down. My move led to a massacre.

12 ♘b5   ♛a5?

This was my last chance of finding some safety for my king, although 12 ... 0-0 would still leave me with some problems.

13 ♘xd6+   ♚e7

14	♛a3	♚f6
15	g4	♗h6+
16	♚b1	♗d7
17	h4	♗f4
18	♛b3!	♗e6
19	♗c4	♗xc4
20	♛xc4	♖f8
21	♘xb7	♛a6
22	♖d6+	

I should have resigned here but eight year olds are less concerned with chess etiquette than the hope of a stalemate.

22	...	♛xd6
23	♘xd6	♘d7
24	♘c3	♘b6
25	♘d5+	♚e6
26	♘xb6+	♚xd6
27	♛d5+	♚c7
28	♘xa8+	♚b8
29	♖d1	♖c8
30	♛xf7	♚xa8
31	♖d7	♖xc2
32	♛d5+	♚b8
33	♛b7 mate	

Eventually Michael finished with 5½ out of 9, just half a point behind his school colleague, Mark Crouse, who collected the £25 prize for the highest score by a Cornish Under 14 player. Mark had always seemed to me the best of the other players at school, although he had not performed well at the Primary Schools event. His rivalry and friendship with Michael over the next few years gave my son's chess a considerable boost.

I was pleasantly surprised by the performance of Mark and Michael in this Under 14 event, but had not anticipated them being invited to London for the Lloyds Bank BCF Junior Squad Championships the following month. Michael had never been to London before, so the invitation was regarded principally as a sight seeing opportunity.

Michael's timetable for this event and many others subsequently makes interesting reading. It began at about 9 o'clock on Friday evening, when we left home to catch the overnight sleeper from Truro at about 10 p.m. We had to leave the sleeper at Paddington by 7.30 a.m. and make our way to the chess venue. After finishing at the chess tournament at about 7 p.m. on the Sunday evening, we had to hang around until 10.30 p.m. when we were permitted to get on the return sleeper, which arrived in Truro at about 7.30 a.m. on Monday morning, which just about gave us time to wash and change before leaving for school at about 8.30 a.m. Looking back, I am amazed to think that we did it so often.

However on the first occasion, we made the most of the early start and saw a few of the famous landmarks, before making our way to Hamley's, the renowned toy shop. At least, I thought, Michael would gain some enjoyment from the weekend. This view was reinforced when we arrived at the chess and I noted that Mark and Michael had been given provisional grades of 77 and 80 respectively, while most of the other competitors in the Under 12 event were well into three figures.

Thus I was somewhat mystified when Michael won his first two games. The title "BCF Junior Squad" had implied that the event would be very strong. When another parent asked me how my child was getting on, I casually remarked that I thought the event would have been stronger. Immediately I wished that I had not made this comment, as the gentleman launched into a tirade about English juniors being the best in the world and that if my son had won his first two games, then he must be a very strong player.

Michael's two wins put him among the top boards, where his inexperience was revealed by Philip Rossiter and later by Gavin Wall. Nevertheless he managed a fifty per cent score, which placed him second equal among the Under Tens. What was perhaps more important than the result was the opportunity that he had been given to mix with some of the country's leading juniors.

Game 4 23.3.80	1	e4	c5
M.Croft (BCF105)-Adams	2	♗c4	♘c6
Lloyds Bank BCF Junior Squad	3	♘f3	g6
Under 12, Round Six	4	♘g5	
Sicilian Defence	A rather primitive combination,		

even for a young player and certainly one with a grade of 105. No doubt, the eight year old across the table was viewed as easy meat rather than a grandmaster in the making.

4	...	e6
5	d3	♗g7
6	♘f3	♘ge7
7	0-0	0-0
8	♖e1	a6

My moves to this point had been natural and strong. This move is alright, but not as good as 8 ... d5, which would have been more direct. Nevertheless the text move had its virtues, in that it tempted my opponent to over-commit himself with so few pieces developed.

9	e5	b5
10	♗b3	♗b7
11	a4	b4

Better here would have been 11 ... d6, when all my pieces would come to life.

12 d4

A bad blunder losing material. 12 ♘bd2 was necessary.

12	...	cxd4
13	♘xd4	♘xe5
14	a5	

Again neglecting his development. More to the point was 14 ♗e3.

| 14 | ... | ♘5c6 |
| 15 | ♘xc6 | dxc6 |

15 ... ♘xc6 was more accurate, after which White would lose the a5 pawn. My move also goes against the basic rule of capturing towards the centre.

16 ♕g4

Rather optimistic. He can hardly hope to conduct a successful attack against my well-defended king with just his queen.

| 16 | ... | c5 |
| 17 | ♕c4 | ♖c8 |

18 c3

Another error, which allows me to net a piece.

18	...	♗d5
19	♕xa6	♗xb3
20	c4	♗c2
21	♕b7	♗xb1
22	♖xb1	♕c7
23	♕xc7	♖xc7

24	♗f4	♖a7
25	♗d6	♖c8
26	♖ed1	♘f5
27	♗f4	♖xa5
	White resigns	

My technique was sufficient to finish the game clinically. The resignation is early for this standard, but, in the long run, the result was never in doubt.

Leonard Barden, manager of the National Junior Squads, took the trouble to speak to Michael and had the foresight to sign a book of his that Michael had bought to remember the occasion, "To Michael Adams, future British junior champion", as well as introducing Michael to John Nunn, who autographed Michael's programme.

There were two further "firsts" for Michael before the year was through. Perhaps I ought to explain here that the chess year runs from September 1st, which is the date for the calculation of age groups. Thus Michael was officially an under eight for the whole of this chapter, even though his eighth birthday occurred during the first event.

He played in his first adult weekend Swiss, when we travelled to Bristol for the Manor Tyres Congress, where Michael played in the Minor section for players with grades under 120. I was very pleased with a result of three wins, one draw and one defeat, as I had anticipated quite wrongly that he would have more trouble with adults than children. His result earned him a prize of a year's subscription to *Chess* magazine.

Game 5   14.6.80
Adams-S.Clayton
Manor Tyres
Minor Section, Round Four
English Opening

1	c4	c5
2	♘f3	♘c6
3	d4	cxd4
4	♘xd4	g6
5	♘c3	♗g7
6	e3	♕b6
7	♘d5	♕d8
8	♗e2	e6

9	♘c3	b6
10	♗f3	♗b7
11	♘db5	♕b8
12	♘d6+	♔f8
13	0-0	♗e5

(see diagram)

14 ♘xf7

Black's opening play has not been the best. I had a clear advantage with the simple 14 ♘xb7, but opted for a more spectacular, but less sound, continuation.

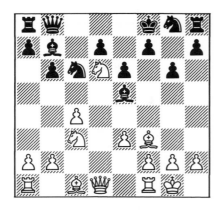

bishop. I am also somewhat hampered by my lack of development and this move allows Black to activate his pieces.

23	...	♘d4
24	♕g4	♗xe4
25	♗e3	♘c2
26	♖ad1	♕c7

If 26 ... ♘xe3 27 ♖d7+. However a better move is 26 ... ♕e8. After the move played, I was able to conclude the game effectively.

14	...	♔xf7
15	♕xd7+	♘ge7
16	♘e4	♖d8

If my opponent had played 16 ... ♗c8, I would have been left with insufficient compensation for my sacrificed material.

17	♘g5+	♔g8
18	♕xe6+	♔h8
19	♘f7+	♔g7
20	♘xd8	♕xd8
21	♗xc6	♘xc6
22	f4	♗f6
23	e4	

It was probably a mistake to have exchanged my light square

27	♖d7+	♕xd7
28	♕xd7+	♔g8
29	♕e6+	♔g7
30	♕xe4	♘xe3
31	♕xa8	♘xf1
32	♕xa7+	♔f8
33	♔xf1	♔g8
34	♕b8+	♔g7
35	♕c7+	♔g8
36	♕xb6	♗g7
37	♕d8+	♗f8
38	c5	♔g7
39	c6	g5
40	c7	♗e7
41	♕xe7+	♔g6
42	c8=♕	gxf4
43	♕g8+	♔f5
44	♕ee6 mate	

Michael found the other "first" even more exciting. This was his first experience of lightning chess, where players have to make their move immediately that a buzzer sounds. He finished fourth equal in the Cornwall Senior event, beating Peggy Clarke, former British Lady Champion along the way.

However her husband, Peter, gained family revenge in the ten minute Holsworthy Quickplay event. Nevertheless Michael did have the honour of playing him on top board in Round Six, after Michael defeated three opponents in excess of 140 BCF grades in successive rounds. He really enjoyed this form of chess, probably because it was the only time that I stopped nagging him about taking more time thinking about his moves.

We had hoped to play one more tournament in the year but unfortunately his entry for the British Under 11 event was rejected as the closing date was passed and we were informed that it would be difficult to run the event with an odd number of players.

It was the only disappointment in the season. If anyone had predicted such happenings in September 1979, I would have not taken them seriously.

3   County Debut

I have divided this book into chapters representing twelve month periods, which coincide with the chess season, where age groups are normally calculated from September 1st. Michael and I have chosen five games to accompany each chapter, so that the reader can obtain some idea of his progress over the years. The games have been chosen, mainly because of their significance in his career. Even so, the choice has been very difficult as Michael has played well over a thousand games that qualify for grading purposes, as well as many quickplay games.

At the beginning of each chess year in September, gradings are issued. These take into account the player's previous grade and all the results of official games that he or she has played in a twelve month period. If, like Michael, the player did not have a previous grade, then it is just calculated from his previous season's results. Like most youngsters, Michael was thrilled to receive his first official grade, which was 101.

This season was a lot busier than the previous one. He played 98 graded games as compared with 31 in the previous year. We travelled to thirteen tournaments outside Cornwall during the course of the new season. In Cornwall, he played more tournaments and league games. This book makes no attempt to cover each tournament or each league fixture. It merely selects some of what I consider the most significant happenings, based on the scrapbooks of newspaper cuttings and scoresheets of all his games that we have kept.

Michael earned a regular place in the Falmouth side during this season, normally appearing on board four. The team had a very good season, finishing second in the league, despite Michael's record of being little better than fifty per cent. This was partly due to the fact that he was playing stronger opposition, who shrewdly worked out Michael's strengths and weaknesses and exploited the latter. Opponents avoided exciting, attacking chess and set out to hold Michael on equal terms until the ending was reached and then take advantage of his inexperience. As the clock was telling a time of about ten o'clock at this stage of the game, it was hard going for a nine year old. However it was a time of learning and Michael rarely repeated the same mistake and by the end of the season, this department of his game had improved considerably.

I have already commented how Michael played far too quickly for my liking and how I constantly nagged him to slow down and concentrate harder. I became quite pleased when his clock times seemed to indicate that my message was beginning to get through, although his facial expression never showed this. I discovered why, when Michael lost a match on time, playing only 13 moves in 90 minutes and finishing in a winning position 23 moves short of the time control. What had happened was that he was letting his clock run to keep me happy and had thought that he had another hour left to reach the time control! I never nagged him about playing too slowly again.

Early in the season I enquired whether there was any chance of Michael playing for Cornwall in the County Championship as I felt that this would be a useful experience, especially as Saturday afternoon seemed a more socially acceptable time for Michael to play his chess. However I was told that his grade of 101 was too low and that he would have to wait at least one more season. Fortunately Falmouth were fixtured with Camborne-Redruth just before the first county match of the season and Michael's opponent was a middle board player in the county second team.

Game 6   26.10.80
Adams-F.T.C.Johns (BCF 125)
Cornish League
Falmouth v. Camborne-Redruth
Board Four
Sicilian Defence

1	e4	c5
2	♘f3	♘c6
3	d4	cxd4
4	♘xd4	♘f6
5	♘c3	d6
6	♗e3	g6
7	♗e2	♗g7
8	♕d2	

I misplaced my bishop on e2 where it does little to improve White's attacking chances. I should have either played f3 instead of ♗e2 prior to castling queenside, or castled kingside at this point.

8	...	0-0
9	0-0-0	♕a5
10	♔b1	♗g4

An inaccurate move. 10 ... ♗d7 or 10 ... ♘xd4 11 ♗xd4 ♗e6 are better continuations. The move played gives White extra time to prepare his attack.

11	f3	♗d7
12	h4	♖fc8
13	♘b3	♕d8
14	g4	♗e6
15	h5	♗xb3

This leaves White with an extremely solid queenside, giving Black few opportunities to attack. Better moves were 15 ... a5 or 15 ... ♘e5, although even then White has a clear advantage.

16	axb3	♔f8
17	hxg6	fxg6
18	♗h6	♗xh6
19	♕xh6+	♔e8
20	g5	♘g8
21	♕xh7	♔d7
22	♘b5	

(see diagram)

Threatening 23 ♖xd6+.

22	...	♕f8
23	♘xd6	

Almost any attack wins from here, but 23 ♖xd6+ ♔e8 24 ♖xg6 should force immediate resignation.

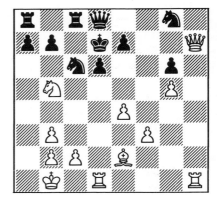

However it is just a matter of technique and mopping up as White exploits the material advantage.

23	...	♔c7
24	♘xc8	♖xc8
25	♕xg6	♘e5
26	♕e6	♕g7
27	f4	♘c6
28	♗g4	♖f8
29	♗f5	♘d4
30	♕c4+	♔b8
31	♖xd4	♕f7
32	♕xf7	♖xf7
33	♖d8+	**Resigns**

After the game, I was told that Michael was playing better than his grade indicated and that he would be included for Saturday's match against Devon. This became a considerable news story as Michael was still only eight and he became the youngest player to represent his county at this level. His photograph appeared in several national newspapers, with stories outlining how his interest in chess had grown out of his interest in toy soldiers.

Game 7 1.11.80
Adams-J.M.Parker (BCF 148)
Cornwall v. Devon
(Second Team Championship)
Giuoco Piano

1	e4	e5
2	♘f3	♘c6
3	♗c4	♗c5
4	c3	♘f6
5	0-0	0-0
6	d4	♗d6
7	d5	

7 ♖e1 is better as Black has tangled up his pieces by playing 5 ... 0-0 instead of 5 ... d6. By blocking the position with the move played, I give him time to untangle them.

7	...	♘e7
8	♖e1	♘g6
9	♘bd2	a5
10	♘f1	♗c5
11	♗e3	♗xe3
12	♘xe3?	

I overlooked the fact that I was losing a pawn. Fortunately, it worked out reasonably well, as there is some compensation.

12	...	♘xe4
13	♗d3	

If 13 ♘f5, Black has a strong reply in 13 ... ♘d6

13	...	♘g5
14	♘xg5	♕xg5

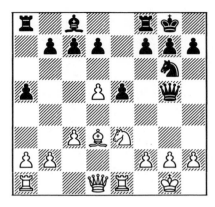

15 d6!

This demonstrates White's compensation for the blundered pawn, although Black still holds the advantage.

15	...	cxd6
16	♗xg6	

If 16 ♘c4, White would have problems meeting a timely ... ♘f4.

16	...	hxg6
17	♕xd6	♖a6
18	♕d5	d6
19	♖ad1	♕e7
20	♕b5	♗e6
21	♘d5	♗xd5
22	♖xd5	♕c7
23	♕e2	♖c6
24	♖ed1	b6

To keep his extra pawn, Black needed to play ♖e8-e6 to avoid being pinned along the d-file. Even then his pieces would be so tied up that it would be difficult to convert the pawn advantage into a win. After the move played, I can regain the pawn with a tactical trick.

	25	♕d3	♖b8

If 25 ... ♖d8 26 ♖xe5.

26	♖xd6	♖xd6
27	♕xd6	♕xd6
28	♖xd6	♔f8
29	♔f1	♔e7
30	♖d3	♔e6
31	♔e2	b5
32	b3	f5
33	f3	♖c8
34	g3	g5
35	g4	

This ending illustrates my lack of knowledge in the endgame at this stage of my career. Black could have won a pawn by 35 ... ♖h8.

36	...	g6
36	♔f2	a4
37	b4	♖c4

38	h3	♖c8
39	a3	♖h8
40	♔g2	♖c8
41	♔h2	♖c4

Black still has winning chances and could have created a passed pawn by 41 ... e4, when it would have been difficult for me to have held the draw. In this ending, I made the mistake of blocking the queenside, where I had a potentially passed pawn, and allowed my king to drift to the side of the board, when it is needed in the centre to cover any pawn break by Black.

42	♔g3	f4+
43	♔f2	♖c8

Black's last chance was to play 43 ... e4, but most of his advantage disappeared when he played 42 ... f4+, which destroyed the flexibility of his pawns in the same way that 37 b4 destroyed White's chances.

44	♔g2	½-½

This result was sufficient to earn him a place in the team whenever he was available for the next few seasons. Whatever other benefits accrued from playing in these games, they certainly helped to develop his stamina. Cornwall did not play any of their fixtures at home, apart from the Devon match in alternate seasons. The rest of their games were played at Exeter or Taunton. That meant at least a 200 mile round journey from our home in Falmouth. By the time you allowed for hold-ups (Cornwall still has no motorways) and waited for the last player in the car to complete his game, something like ten hours or more had passed, all for one game of chess, which Cornwall invariably lost.

As I was seen frequently at chess venues with Michael, it was assumed that I was very interested in the game myself and I was talked into becoming secretary of the Cornwall Secondary Schools League. I did so on the understanding that our junior school would be allowed to take part in the league. I thought that one of the best ways that children would improve their chess was by playing against better players. Therefore it was unfortunate that with Michael and Mark leading the side, we won some of our matches 5-0. However a timely defeat by Redruth School just before the County Primary Schools Congress destroyed the dangers of over-confidence that might have existed and did the children a power of good.

The event had been extended to three age groups, with a separate competition for Under Nines for the first time. Despite a turn-out of twenty-five schools, King Charles' players finished first and second in each event, as well as enjoying other high placings. I decided that Michael should play in his own age group and he duly won the Under Nine event, with Gareth Price and Mark Crouse taking the Under Ten and Under Eleven events respectively.

Michael and Mark went on to share the County Under Thirteen title, both winning their first six games conclusively and agreeing a timid draw in their final round meeting.

The Under Fifteen and Under Eighteen events were held the same weekend. Both were Five round events, but whereas the younger age group played all their games in one day, with half an hour allowed for all of their moves, the Under Eighteen games qualified for grading purposes as they were played at a much slower rate and that competition was spread over two days. Michael had not played in either event previously and we were not sure which event to enter him for. In a silly moment, we decided to enter both events together, as they were being held in adjacent rooms.

This meant that Michael was involved in playing two games simultaneously in separate rooms against two opponents, who were a lot older than himself. Not only that, but both games were played on clocks. You can see why I said it was a silly moment that we decided on this choice. Yet Michael scampered from room to room, anxiously looking to see if it was his move and trying to rationalise his efforts so that he concentrated his efforts on the board where he had the greater problem. He did it so successfully that he only dropped a half point in the first round of the Under 15 event and won the other five "simultaneous" games.

Eventually the younger age group resulted in an eight way tie on four points. Michael and Mark both had a chance of winning it outright but could only draw their games despite the fact that Michael only had one game to worry about then. One other King Charles boy, Carl Mason, figured in the multiple tie, so we were well represented in the play-off some weeks later. Michael triumphed in this play-off.

Strangely enough, the Under 18 event was much easier to win. The decisive victory came in Round Four, when Michael defeated a 146-graded opponent. In so doing, he became the youngest player ever to win a County title in this age group.

Our excursions out of Cornwall were dependent on the venue and the time of the school year. We could get to Devon tournaments in time for a Friday evening first round game in term time, but otherwise tournaments with Friday evening games were restricted to holiday time. We were lucky that there were so many tournaments in Devon at that time. Not only were there Torbay and East Devon, which still continue, but also a Plymouth Christmas Congress and three weekend congresses in Woolacombe organised by Peter Clarke and the Hexagon organisation, all of which sadly no longer take place.

Michael gained a wealth of experience in these Minor tournaments, where he competed against players with grades up to about 130, depending on the particular event. His performances ranged from three out of six for a 102 grading performance up to four and a half out of five for a 154 performance. Games have been chosen from both these events.

His worst performance came at Islington. We were undoubtedly lured by a £150 first prize and calculated that after train fares, an entry fee and Saturday night accommodation in London, a healthy profit could be secured by winning the Under 120 section. Looking back, it was pretty naive thinking. Just because you beat a 125 opponent on one occasion, it does not mean that your are going to beat all players with grades of 125 and less on every occasion, as Michael soon found out.

Game 8 20.12.80	2 ♘c3	♘c6
K.Bracewell (BCF 77)-Adams	3 g3	d6
Islington Minor, Round Two	4 ♗g2	♘f6
Sicilian Defence		

1   e4   c5

A more standard move in a closed Sicilian is 4 ... g6, but this is the first time that I encountered this opening.

5	♘ge2	e6
6	d3	♗e7
7	♗e3	a6

Black's normal plan for queen-side expansion includes playing ... ♖b8, removing it from the a8-h1 diagonal, as after 7 ... a6 8 0-0 b5? 9 e5 wins material.

8	0-0	0-0
9	f4	♘g4
10	♗c1	♕c7
11	h3	♘f6
12	f5	h6?

White's pawn advance in front of his king was something new to me and frightened me into a passive move. A better reply would have been 12 ... b5 gaining space on the queenside and preparing to kick White's knight from c3.

13	♘f4	b5
14	♘h5	

(see diagram)

14 ...   exf5?

Another panic reaction, which lost control of the d5 square. 14 ... b4 was a much stronger move, although White still had the better

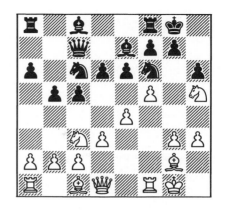

chances.

15	♘xf6+	♗xf6
16	♘d5	♗d4+
17	♔h2	♕d8
18	exf5	♗b7

18 ... ♗d7 should have been played, though even then Black's position is highly undesirable. Following my move, White finished crisply, particularly for a player with a 77 grade.

19	f6	♘b4
20	♕g4	**Resigns**

On this occasion, my resignation may have been a little premature, but if 20 ... g6, White wins a piece with either 21 ♘xb4 or 21 ♘e7+, followed by ♗xb7.

Such a disappointment could have put a less resilient youngster off chess for a considerable time, but five days later, immediately after Christmas, we were off to Plymouth for another event and more disappointment.

Michael's appearance in the county side at the age of eight had resulted in an invitation from the local television company to appear in a news programme. My son was not very enthusiastic about this invitation, despite my urgings that it would be good to see an item about chess on the news. A compromise was reached where it was agreed that Michael would take part in an interview in between the fourth and final rounds. At that stage, Michael had three and a half points out of four and if he won his last round game, he would have become the youngest ever player to win an adult tournament. Naturally the interviewer talked about such a possibility, while the local newspaper carried a headline, "Youngest player poised". When we drove back to the chess venue, TV cameras were present to record the start of the round. Unfortunately Michael was paired with his pal, Mark Crouse. There was to be no cautious draw on this occasion and no glory for Michael either, as Mark won a hard fought game.

Nevertheless it was only a fortnight later that Michael did win an adult competition, when he won the Falmouth Cup, the Cornwall Congress Under 125 competition, winning his first four games and drawing his last round game to clinch success. This was a very pleasing result as it showed that he could cope with the pressure of leading tournaments and hold his own against mature, determined players as in the critical Round Four clash between the two players with perfect scores.

Game 9　　　11.1.81
I.K.Pilling (BCF 122)-**Adams**
Cornwall U-125 (Falmouth Cup)
Round Four
Grünfeld Defence

1	d4	♘f6
2	c4	g6
3	♘c3	d5

I had a brief flirtation with the Grünfeld Defence, while temporarily disenchanted with the Nimzo-Indian, although the latter really suits my style better.

4	e3	♗g7
5	♗d2	c6

Solid but unadventurous. 5 ... 0-0 with the idea of a later ... c5 would be more enterprising.

6	♘f3	♕c7?

It was not very clever to expose my queen. 6 ... 0-0, followed by ... ♗g4, ... e6, ... ♘bd7 is a more normal way to play this kind of position.

7	cxd5	cxd5

8	♖c1	♘c6
9	♗d3	♗d7
10	0-0	0-0
11	h3	e6
12	♘b5	♕d8
13	a3	a6
14	♘c3	♘e8
15	♘e2	♘d6
16	♗c3	♖c8
17	♕c2	♘a5

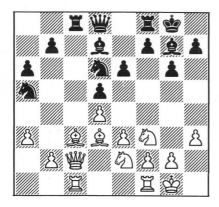

18 e4?

After a prolonged spell of manoeuvring, where neither side has
made progress, White foolishly
decides to break open the centre.
He is ill prepared for this kind of
thrust and should have continued
his manoeuvring by 18 ♕b1, getting himself out of the pin on the
c-file.

18	...	dxe4
19	♗xe4	♘xe4
20	♕xe4	♗c6

21	♕f4	♘c4
22	♘e5	♗b5
23	♖fe1	♘b6
24	♘f3	♘d5
25	♕h4	♕xh4
26	♘xh4	♗xe2
27	♖xe2	♘xc3
28	bxc3	♗xd4
29	c4	♖c5
30	♘f3	♗f6
31	♘d2	♗e7
32	a4	♖d8
33	♘b3	♖c7
34	a5	♖d3
35	♖e3	♖cd7
36	♖c3	♖xc3
37	♖xc3	♗b4
38	♖c2	♖d1+
39	♔h2	♖b1
40	♘d2	♖a1
41	♘b3	♖a3
42	♖b2	♖a4
43	g3	♗c3
44	♖b1	♖xc4
45	♖d1	♖b4
46	♘c5	♖b5
47	♘e4	♗xa5
48	♖d7	♗b4
49	♘g5	♖xg5

White resigns

I can remember feeling pretty
pleased with this game, although
I now realise the opening play was
pretty sloppy. However the technical exploitation of White's mistake in opening the centre was
relentless.

One of the ways of measuring children's progress is by comparing results over successive years in the same event. Thus, his result at the Plymouth Junior Quickplay of seven and a half out of nine was two points to the good. Although he finished in second place, half a point behind John Carlin, he did manage to reverse their individual result from the previous year.

Game 10   22.2.81
J.Carlin-Adams
Plymouth Under 14 Quickplay
Round Eight
Sicilian Defence

1	e4	c5
2	♘f3	d6
3	d4	cxd4
4	♘xd4	♘f6
5	♘c3	a6
6	♗e3	e5
7	♘b3	♗e6
8	f4	♗e7

My first purchase of a book on Black openings was Michael Stean's book on the Sicilian Najdorf. However I was not an avid reader and this is evident as I should have been preventing White playing f5. It was necessary to have played 8 ... exf4.

9	f5	♗xb3

I have to suffer the consequences of allowing f5, either by losing time or giving up the valuable light squared bishop – which is the course I chose.

10	axb3	♘d7

11 ♘d5?

My opponent's middle game plan should have included 11 ♗c4, with domination of the d5 square his aim. I could have played 11 ... ♘xe4, but was wary of 12 ♕g4, although this is not a serious problem after 12 ... ♘df6. The situation would then be unclear, but certainly no worse for Black.

11	...	♘xd5
12	♕xd5	♕c7
13	♗c4	0-0
14	0-0	♘f6
15	♕d2?	

This blunders a pawn that could have been saved by 15 ♕d3.

15	...	♘xe4
16	♕e2	♖ad8
17	♗d3	♕c6
18	♗h6	♘f6
19	♗g5	♖fe8
20	♗xf6	♗xf6
21	c4	

A positionally well motivated move, attempting to gain control of the white squares, but it loses a pawn to a tactical trick.

21	...	♛b6+
22	♔h1	♛xb3
23	♖a3	♛b6
24	♗e4	♖c8
25	♗d5	

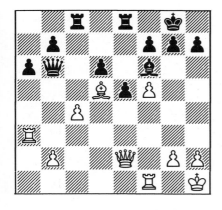

| 25 | ... | e4! |

It is important here that Black does not hang on to material to the extent that his pieces become ineffective. This move activates the bishop on f6, as well as making the passed e-pawn into a threatening weapon. Realising this, White begins to mount an attack on the kingside, using his powerfully placed bishop on d5.

| 26 | ♛h5 | ♖e7 |

26 ... ♖c7 would have been safer as Black's king then has the option of fleeing via f8 to e7.

27	♖h3	h6
28	♛g6	♔f8
29	♛h7	♔e8

It is clear that White's kingside attack is not going to progress very far and Black's extra material should prevail.

| 30 | g4 | |

Desperation, accompanied by a draw offer, which was politely declined.

| 30 | ... | e3 |
| 31 | ♖e1 | e2 |

Today, I would play 31 ... ♔d7, keeping more control of the situation and leaving White's queen stranded. My move was just sufficient for victory.

32	♗xf7+	♔xf7
33	♖xh6	♛f2
34	♛g6+	♔g8
35	♛h7+	♔f8
36	♖xf6+	gxf6
37	♛h8+	♔f7
38	♛h7+	♔e8
39	♛g8+	♔d7
	White resigns	

Apart from the error in giving up the white square bishop in the opening, I was pleased with this competent and sensible performance. Of course, unlike the game against K.Bracewell, I had previous experience of this structure.

His second appearance at the Lloyds Bank Junior Squad Under 12 event resulted in another substantial improvement as he scored five out of seven, with a win against one of the pre-tournament favourites, Mark Wheeler, who had a grade of 162. Michael and Mark Crouse finished sixth equal out of the 110 selected players. Michael Hennigan dominated the event to win with a perfect score, one and a half points ahead of the second placed group.

Michael played in the British Chess Championships for the first time. The congress was held in Morecambe and Michael played in the Under Eleven section. Without doubt, this was the most enjoyable chess experience of Michael's career to this point. He was fortunate that a small amount of money had been allocated to enable him to receive some coaching from Shaun Taulbut, one of our leading players, who was playing in the British Championship. Not only did Shaun find time to do some coaching with Michael, he also introduced him to some of our leading players, such as Nigel Short and Murray Chandler, whose autographs Michael collected.

He led the Under Eleven event for the whole tournament before being overtaken in the final round. He began with four wins, but could only draw his last three games against S.Clarke, Darren Wheeler (the eventual champion) and Ali Mortazavi, which meant that he finished in second equal position. Nevertheless the result offered further confirmation that Michael was among the top players in his age group and we hoped that one day he might win the event.

4 British Under Eleven Champion

Michael's grade for the new season was 127, which necessitated him playing in the Major section of tournaments as the limit for Minor events is usually about 120 and juniors commonly have to add ten points to their grade when deciding which category to enter as they are improving at a faster rate than adults. I have noticed that there is a tendency for some youngsters to be entered for sections higher than they have to, as it gives them a chance to make a name for themselves and there is little pressure on them as so little is expected. We considered it best to play in the section appropriate for his grade, as we reasoned that pressure was not necessarily a bad thing and we reckoned that there would be plenty of time for Opens in a few more years.

I began to play competitively during this season. I felt that this would help me to become a better chess teacher at school. It also stopped me worrying about Michael's play. I have already expressed my concerns about his clock handling. My other main frustration was his habit of spending a lot of time gazing around the room, when he was due to move. I was always tempted to turn his head back towards the board, which would have been against the rules, as it constituted giving help. Some people said that he had no need to look at the board, as he carried the position in his head, but I was not convinced by this argument. Anyway by playing among the lower boards of the Minor, while Michael battled away on the top boards of the Major, it left me in the ideal position – not too far away if needed, but not fussing around his board.

At Falmouth Chess Club, several players had left or retired from competitive chess and Michael moved up to number two board, while I became captain as no one else would take the job on and I sometimes filled in on the lower boards. Also, I was able to introduce other youngsters from school into the Falmouth first team, while several others played for the second team. Probably our best result of the season was a 3-3 draw away to Camborne-Redruth, the eventual champions, with four children under 11 in the side. Michael had a much better record this season, with seven wins and six draws from his fifteen games, with defeats only against Ken Lloyd (BCF 189) and Chris Tylor (BCF 127), giving him a grading performance of 152 and helping the team achieve mid-table respectability.

My chess knowledge had increased to the point that I had discovered that there was a National Primary Schools team competition, so I decided to enter and see how many rounds we could get through. We had lost Mark Crouse, who had transferred to Secondary School, but we had more strength in depth and this was a tribute to the teaching ability of Michael, as well as the willingness of the children to learn. I had introduced the BCF Certificates of Merit scheme in school and the children were really enthusiastic about it. While I was involved teaching the preliminary group, Michael taught the intermediate group and went on to pass the higher level himself, although never taking the advanced level. He was a very good teacher as long as children wanted to learn and I made sure that only those who did worked with him. They learned so fast that we won six rounds to win the western zone and reach the semi-finals, with all our winning margins either 4-1 or better. We found it harder going in London, but narrowly reached the final by winning on board count, with Gareth Price our only winner and Michael clinching victory by holding Gary Quillan to a draw. In the final, our middle three boards were all losing at one stage and I feared the worst, but two of them managed to turn things around and we eventually won 3½-1½ to become the national champions.

Even more remarkable than this was that we won the Cornwall Secondary Schools title. The team were now in their second season in this competition and were never overawed by their opponents, no matter how big they were or whatever their reputation. It is true that we won the two decisive games against Truro School and St. Austell Sixth Form College on board count, but nine successive wins, with Michael winning all his games, was a record that spoke for itself. Incidentally the team was Michael, Gareth Price, Carl Mason, Simon Gay and Piran Trezise. Sadly, I think that Michael is the only one still playing competitively.

Michael was remarkably consistent in his Major competitions, usually registering about seventy per cent. He only won one Major competition and that was part of a quadruple tie at Plymouth, where the leaders scored four and a half out of six. The most amazing occurrence at this congress was the spontaneous round of applause that broke out at the end of his game with Yannick Colliou, the French Under 11 champion, when

Michael held a difficult rook and pawns ending in a quickplay finish. I am not sure what other players thought, but nobody seemed to mind.

One player that kept on crossing Michael's path was Devon's leading Under 11, Jonathon Hutchings. Michael had shared the Devon Under 11 open title with him the previous season and the result was repeated this year. For good measure, they also shared first place at the Plymouth Junior Under 14 quickplay event. In all of these competitions, they beat all their other opponents and drew their individual games. It was becoming clear that Jonathon was going to be a major threat to Michael and the others at the British Under 11 event, which was to be held in Jonathon's home town of Torquay.

Another first equal result came at Lloyds Bank Junior squad Under 12 event, where Colin Davis, an Australian, finished on six and a half out of seven with Michael, although my son was awarded the title on tie break. Thus his score had progressed from three and a half to five and then to six and a half in three successive seasons. For good measure, he shared second equal in the equivalent Under 14 event, where he had to concede a half point bye in Round One, as it was played on Friday evening. He also lost to A.D.Diamond, but scored a pleasing four and a half out of six in an event won by Philip Morris.

As Michael had won the Falmouth Cup in the previous year's competition, he played in the senior county championship, the Emigrant Cup, at the Cornwall Congress. Peter Clarke had won the event for the last five years, but chose not to defend his title. Not that we were contemplating Michael winning the event, which was just as well as he lost his first round game against Dave Barnes (BCF 150). However he surprised most people, including me, to record three wins and a draw in the following rounds to finish in second equal position.

Game 11   4.4.82
R.Grime (BCF 169)-Adams
Cornwall Championship
Round Four
Trompowski Attack

1	d4	♘f6
2	♗g5	d5
3	♘d2	♗f5
4	c3	♘bd7
5	g3	e6
6	♗g2	♗e7
7	♘gf3	h6
8	♗xf6	♘xf6
9	0-0	0-0

The opening is concluded and White cannot be satisfied with his achievements. He has given up the bishop pair, without significant justification.

| 10 | ♖e1 | c5 |
| 11 | ♘b3 | c4?! |

11 ... cxd4 would have opened the game for my two bishops and would have been a stronger continuation. Closing the game suited my opponent, as his knights become more valuable in the blocked position.

12	♘bd2	b5
13	♘e5	♗d6
14	e4	♗h7

A more natural reaction might have been to exchange pieces on e4 but my move was consistent with my strategy of queenside expansion and keeping the tension in the centre.

15 ♘g4?

This loses a pawn for no reason. 15 exd5 was required and I would probably have replied 15 ... ♘xd5, with a balanced game in prospect.

15	...	♘xe4
16	♘xe4	♗xe4
17	♗xe4	dxe4
18	♘e5	

Not 18 ♖xe4? f5

| 18 | ... | f5 |
| 19 | ♘g6 | |

It was better to have started

action on the queenside immediately with 19 b3 or 19 a4.

19	...	♖f6
20	♘h4	♕b6
21	b3	♕c6
22	b4?!	

This closes the queenside which does not help White, especially if Black responds 22 ... a5.

22	...	♖d8?!
23	a4	a6
24	axb5	axb5
25	♖a3	♖a8
26	♖xa8+	♕xa8
27	♕a1	♖f8
28	f3	

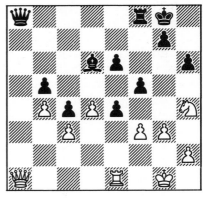

| 28 | ... | ♕b8! |
| 29 | ♕a6 | |

If instead, 29 fxe4 ♗xg3 30 hxg3 ♕xg3+ 31 ♘g2 f4

29	...	♖f6
30	fxe4	♗xg3
31	e5	♗xe1

32	exf6	♗xh4
33	♕xe6+	♔h8
34	f7	♕f8
35	d5	♗e7
36	♔f2	♔h7
37	h4	

I am threatening to win the pawn on f7 by g6, followed by ♔g7 and ♕xf7.

37	...	♗xh4+
38	♔f3	g6
39	d6	♔g7
40	♕e5+	♗f6

41	♕xb5	♕xf7
42	d7	g5
43	♕xf5	♗d8
44	♕xf7+	♔xf7

White resigns

This was a somewhat scrappy game, played among the middle boards, where my opponent probably had less ambition than me. However, it was a landmark at the time, as I had never beaten anyone with such a high grade previously in a graded game.

Michael has been fortunate enough to meet and play many famous chess players in his short career. One of the first of them was A.R.B.Thomas, who beat him in their first encounter.

Game 12   1.5.82
Adams-A.R.B.Thomas (BCF 193)
Taw Tournament Round Three
Two Knights Defence

1	e4	e5
2	♘f3	♘c6
3	d4	exd4
4	♗c4	♘f6
5	e5	d5
6	♗b5	♘e4
7	♘xd4	♗d7
8	♗xc6	bxc6
9	0-0	♗c5
10	f3	♘g5
11	♘c3	

I played the Scotch Gambit for well over a year, which included my two appearances in the BCF Under 11 events. It brought me a lot of success, although not on this occasion. 11 f4 was a better move and would not have allowed Black to have obtained such a comfortable position from the opening.

11	...	♘e6
12	♗e3	♗xd4
13	♗xd4	c5
14	♗f2	♗c6
15	♕d2	0-0
16	♘e2	d4

(see diagram)

| 17 | ♖ad1? | |

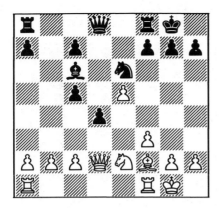

It was silly to open the position as my opponent had superior minor pieces. However, if I had closed the centre by playing 17 c4, I would have had a perfectly reasonable game. The redundant knight on e2 could then be brought to d3 via c1, focusing on Black's weakened queenside. This move would also have taken away the d5 square from the black pieces.

17	...	♕d5
18	c3	♗b5
19	♗g3	♕xa2

This was a direct result of my failure to play c4. I have lost a pawn and my opponent's pieces are still dominant.

20	cxd4	♗xe2
21	♕xe2	♘xd4
22	♕f2	♖ab8
23	♖d2	♖b3
24	♖c1	

24 e6!.

24	...	♖fb8
25	♖xc5	♖xb2
26	♖xb2	♖xb2
27	♖xc7	♖b1+
28	♕f1	♘e2+
29	♔f2	♖xf1+
30	♔xf1	♘xg3+
31	hxg3	g5
32	♖c8+	♔g7
33	♖c7	♕b1+
34	♔e2	♕b2+
35	♔f1	♕b5+
36	♔f2	♕b6+

White resigns

This was a very clinical finish by a fine player, who never gave me a chance to recover from the mistakes that I made earlier in the game. My opponent was kind enough to write a generous letter of encouragement to me, with his own comments about the game.

Another good tournament result was recorded in the Manor Tyres Major, where Michael was one of seven players in equal second position. His tournament performance was equivalent to a 176 grading performance, which along with his Cornwall Congress result was his best so far.

Game 13   28.6.82
Adams-A.Hibbit (BCF 154)
Manor Tyres Major
Round Five
Pirc Defence

1	e4	d6
2	d4	♘f6
3	♘c3	g6
4	f3	

It would have been better to have maintained more flexibility with 4 ♗e3, as f3 loses time in some variations.

4	...	♗g7
5	♗e3	0-0
6	♕d2	c6
7	h4	e5
8	♘ge2	exd4
9	♗xd4	

More natural, and better, would have been 9 ♘xd4. The bishop occupies a somewhat exposed post at d4 and impedes the smooth development of my kingside.

9	...	d5
10	exd5	

The exposed nature of the bishop would have been revealed in the variation 10 e5 ♘fd7 11 h5 c5

10	...	cxd5
11	0-0-0	♘c6
12	♗e3	♗e6
13	♔b1	♕a5
14	♘d4	♖ac8
15	g4	♖fe8

16	♗f2	♘e5
17	h5	♘c4?

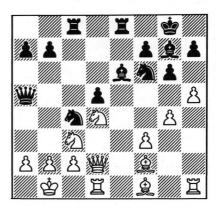

Both sides have developed fairly naturally, although White's attack is likely to be quicker. A pawn storm on the queenside by Black is likely to be too slow to be effective. Thus, he should seek to find counterplay using his pieces, although it is not clear how. Exchanging his well placed knight on e5 for my undeveloped bishop on f1 is clearly a mistake.

18	♗xc4	♖xc4
19	hxg6	fxg6
20	♖he1	♗f7
21	♖xe8+	♘xe8
22	♕d3	♘d6
23	♘b3	♕a6
24	♘xd5	

Although Black has managed to take the sting out of my kingside attack, his other weakness, the isolated d-pawn, has been exposed.

24	...	♖a4
25	♕xa6	♖xa6
26	♘b4	♖a4

Black's pieces are already in trouble through their lack of co-ordination. Now my opponent loses further material by force.

27	♖xd6	♖xb4
28	♖d8+	♗e8
29	♖xe8+	♔f7
30	♖d8	♖f4
31	♖d3	a6

32	c3	b5
33	♘c5	a5
34	♖d7+	♔g8
35	♖xg7+	**Resigns**

I still feel quite pleased with this game. One of the most difficult things to achieve in chess is to switch the attack from one target to another. This was a smooth performance in switching from the kingside attack to pressure against a poor pawn structure.

This was his last longplay tournament before the British Championships and put us in good heart. I had high hopes that he might win the Under 11 event, but we never spoke about it for fear of creating unnecessary pressure. Margaret and Janet joined us for the week at Torquay and, with the exception of Edinburgh, this was repeated every year up to Swansea. Living in Cornwall and having two children, who were not the best of travellers, we had not looked to go very far. However once Michael became involved with the British Championships, we did not like the idea of a divided family, so we built a holiday around the chess like many other families. It resulted in Michael spending a little less time around the chess hall, but more importantly, it resulted in him having more fresh air and exercise, not to mention an improved diet, as we always went self-catering.

The week began well with Michael managing to obtain a place in the open-air simul against his first International Master opponent, Jim Plaskett, and winning a free BCF T-shirt by virtue of this result.

Game 14   1.8.82
Adams-J.Plaskett (BCF 232)
"Chess in the Sun" Simultaneous
Sicilian Defence

1	e4	c5

2	♘f3	d6
3	d4	cxd4
4	♘xd4	♘f6
5	♘c3	a6
6	♗g5	e6
7	f4	b5

Few masters would be brave enough to play this extremely sharp variation in a simultaneous display, but Jim Plaskett is renowned for his uncompromising play. Even so, it is doubtful that he had any idea of my ability.

8	e5	dxe5
9	fxe5	♛c7
10	♛e2	♞fd7
11	0-0-0	♝b7
12	♞f3	

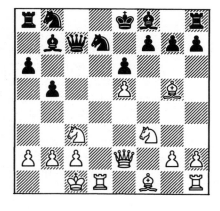

This is not the most critical test of the variation. A great deal of analysis of other moves such as 12 ♛g4 and 12 ♛h5 has been made.

12	...	♞c5?

An unfortunate blunder, which can happen when giving a simultaneous, as I know only too well! It means that the game is over, almost before it has begun. 12 ... ♞c6 was of course much better.

13	♜d8+	♛xd8
14	♝xd8	♚xd8
15	♞g5	

The loss of material need not be fatal for Black, but the undeveloped state of his forces means that he goes under to a direct attack.

15	...	♚e8
16	♛f2	b4
17	♛xf7+	♚d8
18	♝c4	bxc3
19	♞xe6+	♞xe6
20	♜d1+	**Resigns**

There was a certain amount of criticism about our decision to enter the Under 11 event and many thought that Michael should have played in an older age group. However we knew that it was never easy to win an event, whereas it was comparatively easy to be well placed. What we wanted to know was whether Michael was good enough to be a winner. There were several players capable of causing an upset, although we thought the big test would be when he came up against Jonathon. This happened in Round Five, when they entered the round as the only two players with perfect scores, although to do so, Michael had beaten two players that he had previously only drawn against.

Game 15   4.8.82
Adams-J.Hutchings (BCF 96)
British Under 11
Round Five
Sicilian Defence

1	e4	c5
2	♘f3	d6
3	d4	cxd4
4	♘xd4	♘f6
5	♘c3	a6
6	♗g5	e6
7	f4	♗e7
8	♕f3	

In my youth, I was keener to enter the sharpest opening variations. Nowadays, I prefer to avoid heavily analysed lines.

8	...	♕c7
9	0-0-0	♘c6
10	♘b3	

A more critical test of this system is 10 ♘xc6 bxc6 11 e5 with complex play.

10	...	♖b8
11	♗d3	b5
12	♖he1	♗b7
13	♕g3	♖c8

My opponent has wasted time, moving the rook from a8 to b8 and c8 and this allows me to launch a powerful attack in the centre. Better was 13 ... b4, driving my knight to a more passive square.

14	e5	dxe5
15	fxe5	♘h5
16	♕g4	g6

17	♗xe7	♘xe7
18	♕g5	h6
19	♕d2	♘g7
20	♕f2	

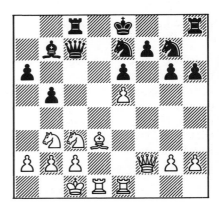

20	...	♘gf5

Better was 20 ... 0-0 but Black's passive knights and weakened kingside means that he stands worse anyway. The move played allows a neat combination that is quite common in Sicilian positions.

21	g4	♘g7
22	♗xb5+	♘c6

If 22 ... axb5 23 ♘xb5 is total disaster for Black.

23	♗xc6+	♗xc6
24	♕f6	0-0
25	♕h4	♔h7
26	♘d4	♗a8
27	♖d3	♖h8
28	♕f6	♘e8
29	♕f4	♔g7
30	h4	♕e7

31	h5	g5
32	♕d2	♖c7
33	♖d1	♕c5
34	♕e3	♕b4
35	♖3d2	♖b7
36	b3	♖c7
37	♔b2	a5
38	♕d3	♗c6?

Black has put up spirited resistance, but the weakness of his king's position and the pawn disadvantage should prove too much. His last move allows a neat trick and makes the task of winning much easier.

39	♘xe6+	♔g8
40	♘xc7	♘xc7

41	♕d8+	♘e8
42	♘d5	♕b5
43	♘f6+	♔g7
44	♘xe8+	♖xe8
45	♕f6+	♔g8
46	♖d8	a4
47	♖xe8+	♗xe8
48	♖d8	axb3
49	axb3	♔f8
50	e6	**Resigns**

It was a relief to beat Jonathon at the fourth attempt. I knew that I had to attack to do so, without taking too many risks in such a crucial game. I seem to have got the right balance in giving a good, solid performance.

Although there were three rounds to go, we sensed that the championship was Michael's. Two more quick wins ensured that it was, while a final round success meant that he had become the first player to win an age group event at the championships with a perfect score. Whatever else lay ahead of him in chess, it was a nice feeling that he would always be able to say that he was once the British Under 11 champion.

5 International Recognition

Michael began his last year at King Charles Junior School with a grade of 155. It sounds fine, until you remember he was still an under eleven for this season. Yet he was forced to play in Opens, because of his high grade. I feel sure that he would have benefited from another season of Majors to see if he was capable of winning such events, but on the other hand he would have to move up to Opens sometime and it could be argued that the sooner he made the move the better.

Most of the time was spent battling among the middle boards of Opens, struggling to overcome experienced players of about 170 grade and often failing. On the few occasions that the Major limit was as high as 170, he entered that section, but still found wins hard to come by, with a very high percentage of draws on his record. He was fortunate that he also had age group events as well as local chess to compete in and his record there was much better. However wins like this in Open events were few and far between.

Game 16   9.10.82
Adams-G.Miller (BCF 161)
Golden Coast Tournament
Round Three
Sicilian Defence

1	e4	c5
2	♘f3	d6
3	d4	cxd4
4	♘xd4	♘f6
5	♘c3	a6
6	♗g5	e6
7	f4	b5
8	e5	dxe5

9	fxe5	♛c7
10	♛e2	♘fd7
11	0-0-0	♗b7
12	♛g4	

My main use of books was after I had played a game and looked up how I could have improved. After my game with Plaskett, I consulted Stean's book to confirm that 12 ♘f3 was not a particularly critical line.

12	...	♛xe5
13	♗d3	h6

42

13 ... h5 would be refuted by 14 ♕xe6+ and if 14 ... fxe6, then 15 ♗g6 mates.

14	♘xe6!	hxg5
15	♖he1	♘f6

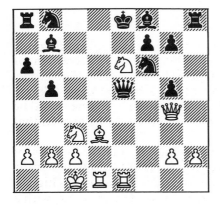

The Polugayevsky variation of

the Sicilian is very double-edged and when entering into it, Black takes a considerable risk unless he has all the latest knowledge at his fingertips.

16 ♗xb5+!

After this move, Black is lost as after 16 ... axb5 17 ♘c7+ ♔e7 18 ♖xe5 is mate.

16	...	♘bd7
17	♗xd7+	♘xd7
18	♘c7+	♔e7
19	♕xd7+	♔f6
20	♖xe5	♔xe5
21	♖e1+	♔f6
22	♖f1+	♔g6
23	♕xf7+	♔h6
24	♘xa8	♗b4
25	g4	**Resigns**

Unfortunately, Michael's period of coaching from Shaun Taulbut came to an end after the British Championships at Torquay. It was not possible for the financial arrangements to be renewed, which was a great pity as it coincided with a time when Michael needed all the help that was going. The geographical isolation of Cornwall and the shortage of top class players in the area made it impossible for me to organise coaching for him at this stage of his career, although it would be wrong if I did not acknowledge the encouragement and help given by locals like Michael Prettejohn, Don McFarlane and Philip Williams among others, at an earlier stage.

Meanwhile I cannot praise Shaun too highly for the help that he was to Michael. In subsequent years, several people had brief spells of working with Michael but the arrangements never proved as satisfactory. I think it is a great shame that there is no professional chess player to take charge of our juniors in the same way as there is in some continental countries, although I realise that insufficient income is the reason for it. Anyway at Plymouth, pupil met master and there was no confusion of roles.

Game 17   29.12.82
Adams-S.Taulbut (BCF 232)
Plymouth Open
Round Three
Caro Kann Defence

1	e4	c6
2	d4	d5
3	♘d2	dxe4
4	♘xe4	♘d7
5	♗c4	♘gf6
6	♘g5	e6
7	♕e2	♘b6
8	♗d3	h6
9	♘5f3	c5
10	dxc5	♘bd7
11	c6	

Theory concentrates on 11 b4 b6 12 ♘d4, with complicated play. The move played allows Black comfortable equality.

11	...	bxc6
12	♘h3	

This mobilisation of White's forces is not successful. Better was the modest 12 ♘d2, which ensures a more harmonious development. Shaun Taulbut neatly takes advantage of this slip.

12	...	g5!
13	♘hg1	♗g7
14	♘d2	0-0
15	♘gf3	♘d5

16	♘b3	a5
17	a4	♘b4
18	0-0	♘xd3
19	cxd3	♖b8
20	♕c2	♕b6
21	♘bd2	♗a6
22	♖a3	♕c5
23	♘c4	♖fc8
24	♗e3	♕d5
25	b3	f5
26	h3	e5

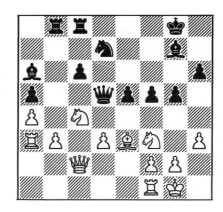

27 ♕e2?

After making a mess of the opening, I have fought back well to reach an unclear position. Although Black has good attacking prospects he also has some weaknesses. Probably 27 ♖e1 is the correct move, removing the piece from the a6-f1 diagonal. The move played deserves to lose for tactical reasons, putting another piece on the diagonal. However it is also a positional mistake.

27	...	♝f8
28	♖fa1	

Also completely hopeless was ♖3a1.

28	...	♝xa3
29	♖xa3	f4
30	♝c1	♖e8
31	♘fd2	♘c5
32	♝b2	♖e6
33	♝c3	♛xd3

34	♛xd3	♘xd3
35	♝xa5	e4
36	♝b6	c5
37	a5	e3
38	fxe3	fxe3

White resigns

This was my first match against a titled player in a graded game and it was disappointing not to do better, particularly against Shaun. The result was decided by one poor move, just when the game was becoming interesting. After that, there was no coming back against a player of Shaun's calibre.

Michael's Cornish league record indicated that he was still improving and the eleven wins and three draws from sixteen games on Board One for Falmouth gave him a grading performance of 173. Only Hugh Coleman (BCF 192), reigning county champion, had the better of him over two games, with a win and a draw, although Brian Parkin (BCF 142) also recorded a win against Michael.

The school season seemed an anti-climax after the triumphs of the previous season. Only Michael was left from that team and the newcomers were not only inexperienced but rather overawed at the prospect of playing in the same team as Michael. They were content to win age group events in the county, but never really expected to beat Secondary School opponents, although I suppose it was a bit daunting when our first match was against the local comprehensive and we had to face five of our former pupils. We did reach round five of the national championships but then went out on board count to a Bristol school.

Michael was delighted to receive his first international recognition when he was selected to captain England Primary Schools against their Scottish counterparts. England won the match by 70 to 10 and Michael won both of his games. It is interesting to look at the names in the English side, which contained Mark Walker, Graeme Buckley and Edward Holland, but also several that I have not heard of in recent years, so I assume that they no longer play competitively.

A much more difficult assignment was presented to him when he was invited to play in the Lloyds Bank Junior International event, which was held at Ken Butt's house at Plymouth. It was rather like the continuation of the struggle in the Opens, with five hard fought draws among his seven games contributing to a fifty per cent score in an event won by the Dane, Henrik Danielsen. Still I felt that it was a very good result in a very strong field, especially when it is remembered that he was by far the youngest player.

Having played the last round in the morning in Plymouth and attended the prizegiving, Michael dashed back to Falmouth in time to travel to the first round of the Cornwall Congress the same evening. It made it all worthwhile when he finished first equal in the Emigrant Cup with Aelred Horn and Ian George with three wins each and draws between them. Unfortunately the play-off was never arranged, so it was questionable whether he had become the youngest ever county champion. While it is certainly true that Cornwall has never been a strong chess playing county, events still have to be won and results like this provided great encouragement in this particular season.

One of the strangest games that he played during this season was against Philip Walden. Their second round clash occurred on Saturday morning and as my opponent had not turned up, I was strolling around the playing area, trying to look nonchalant when I noticed that their game had begun, but no one was seated at the board. When I noticed that it was Michael's clock that was running, I was not surprised, as I have already mentioned his inclination to be interested in other events than his own game. While I was looking around and wondering where he was, Philip came up to tell me that Michael had blundered and was going to lose a piece and had disappeared from sight. When I eventually found him and tried to console him, I suggested that perhaps he should resign and ask his opponent whether he would be prepared to play a friendly so that Michael might get some benefit from the pairing. This idea was not well received, so I pointed out that the only alternative was to return to the board and play some moves.

Game 18 30.4.83		1	d4	♘f6
P.Walden (BCF 190)-Adams		2	c4	e6
Taw Tournament, Round Two		3	g3	♗b4+
Bogoljubow-Indian Defence		4	♘d2	d6

5 ♗g2   e5?

A terrible blunder, which is a standard trick in this variation. My only excuse is that I had not encountered it previously.

6 ♕a4+   ♘c6
7 ♗xc6+

Much simpler was 7 d5, which wins the piece without the loss of the white squared bishop.

7 ...   bxc6
8 ♕xb4   exd4
9 c5!

I might well have resigned, if my opponent had played 7 d5. However his handicaps of the absence of a light squared bishop and being behind in development gave me some hope. If he had played 9 ♘gf3, things would have been even more difficult for him, as I would have replied 9 ... c5 and kept the extra pawn.

9 ...   0-0
10 ♕xd4   ♕e7
11 ♘b3   h6
12 ♗f4   ♖b8
13 ♖d1   ♘d5
14 f3

The major problem for White has been that ♘f3 can be answered powerfully by ... ♗h3, when White's king is no nearer safety.

14 ...   ♖e8
15 cxd6

Probably better was 15 ♔f2 immediately, retaining the option of taking on d6 at a later stage if necessary. White should be in no hurry to make this capture, as it gives Black's pawn centre more mobility.

15 ...   cxd6
16 ♔f2   ♗a6
17 ♗d2   ♕e6
18 e4   ♘f6
19 ♗c3   ♖bd8
20 h4   c5
21 ♕d2

With hindsight, 21 ♕e3 was the correct continuation. However it was difficult to predict the sacrifice that follows.

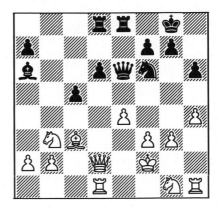

21 ...   ♘xe4+!
22 fxe4   ♕xe4

Although I am two pieces for two pawns down, my pieces are more active and having a light squared bishop is a great asset.

With best play, White should still be winning, but that rarely happens in the tension of a game, especially when players are running short of time.

23   ♖h2

White could have played more effectively with 23 ♘f3 continuing 23 ... ♗b7 24 ♕d3 or 23 ... ♗e2 24 ♕f4.

23	...	♕f5+
24	♕f4	♕c2+
25	♖d2	

White was desperately short of time and should have considered repeating the position once by 25 ♕d2, thus drawing closer to the time control.

25	...	♕b1
26	♘e2	♖e4
27	♕f3	♖de8
28	♘bc1	d5
29	♗a5	♖4e5

30   ♘d3

If 30 ♖xd5 ♖xe2+ 31 ♘xe2 ♖xe2+ 32 ♕xe2 ♗xe2 33 ♔xe2 ♕e4+ wins for Black.

30	...	♖e3
31	♕xe3	♖xe3
32	♔xe3	d4+
33	♘xd4	cxd4+
34	♔xd4	♗xd3
35	♗c3	♗b5
36	♔e3	♕e1+
37	♔f4	♔h7
38	a3	f5

Black holds an advantage in this position, but this move seriously weakens my king position, after which a draw is inevitable.

39	♔xf5	♕xg3
40	♖hg2	♕f3+
41	♔e6	♗c4+
42	♔d6	♕f8+
43	♔c7	♕c5+
44	♔d8	♕f8+
45	♔c7	½-½

Another strange occurrence happened at the East Devon Open during the first round game on Friday evening. I was struggling with a lost game in the opening round when I was aware of a large crowd around Michael's board after about three hours of play. I did not go across and it was only later that I found out that Michael had fallen asleep at the board. Nobody knew what to do because it was felt that if I was asked to wake him up, it would constitute receiving help from a third party, which would be against the laws of chess. As it happened, Michael stirred after a quarter hour or so and proceeded to play a move as if nothing had happened. Bearing in mind his age and the fact that he had spent a day in school, rushed home to change and grab a bite to eat and then been driven all the way to Exeter, it was surprising it had not happened on other occasions.

As we had won the National Primary School Championships the previous year, children from the school were invited to appear on the "Play Chess" television programme with Bill Hartston. Both Michael and Janet appeared on the series, but there was no doubt that my daughter enjoyed it more. She insisted on appearing in front of the cameras with her cuddly panda and was encouraged to do so by Bill. Michael would have preferred to be at a chess congress than answering a question such as how he worked at improving his chess. When he commented that he always went through games that he had lost, it seemed an innocent remark, although it did not seem it later in the year.

The two top players in Cornwall and Devon at this time were Peter Clarke and Gary Lane and it was heartening that Michael beat them both in this season in quickplay events. While I do not imagine there was the slightest chance of this happening at a slower rate, it was another indicator of Michael's potential.

He had already drawn with Gary in the October Plymouth Quickplay and had in fact been winning when he suggested the draw, possibly being rather overawed by the possibility of beating such a strong opponent. However Michael made no mistake the second time around.

Game 19   6.2.83
G.Lane (BCF 207)-**Adams**
Plymouth Quickplay
Round Three
Caro Kann Defence

1	e4	c6
2	d4	d5
3	e5	♗f5
4	h4	h5
5	c4	e6
6	♘c3	♘d7
7	cxd5	cxd5
8	♗g5	♗e7
9	♕d2	a6

10	♗e2	♖c8
11	♘f3	g6

An inaccurate move. 11 ... ♘h6 was better.

12	0-0	♗xg5
13	♘xg5	♘e7
14	f3	f6

The darker side of 11 ... g6 is revealed. The bishop on f5 is rather short of squares.

15	exf6	♘xf6
16	g4	hxg4
17	fxg4	♖xh4

18	gxf5	exf5
19	♖f4	

Although White has won a piece, his kingside has been opened up and that is highly significant in a half-hour game, where king safety is of great importance.

19	...	♖h8

Better was 19 ... ♕d6 with the idea of 20 ♖xh4 ♕g3+

20	♖af1	♘e4
21	♘gxe4	dxe4
22	♗d1	♖h3
23	♗e2	

23 ♘xe4, although looking strong, is answered by 23 ... ♘d5, with an unclear position.

23	...	e3
24	♕e1	♖xc3!
25	bxc3	♘d5

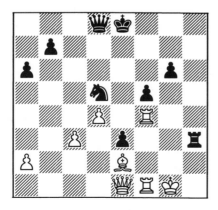

26	♖xf5	

The enormous threat of ... ♕g5+ is difficult to counter. White is forced to return his material advantage, but Black's attack is not yet over.

26	...	gxf5
27	♖xf5	♕d6
28	♗h5+	♖xh5!

After this move, the game is essentially decided, although I took far too long on the mopping up process.

29	♖xh5	♕g6+
30	♔f1	♕xh5
31	♕g3	♕f5+
32	♔e1	♕b1+

Simpler was 32 ... ♕f2+, forcing the exchange of queens.

33	♔e2	♕c2+
34	♔f3	♕d1+
35	♔e4	♘xc3+
36	♔xe3	♕e2+
37	♔f4	♘d5+
38	♔g5	♕e3+
39	♕xe3	♘xe3
40	♔f4	♘d5+
41	♔e5	♘c3
42	a3	♔d7
43	d5	♘b1
44	a4	♘c3
45	a5	♘a2
46	♔d4	♔d6
47	♔c4	♘c1
48	♔d4	♘b3+
49	♔c4	♘xa5+
50	♔b4	♔xd5

51	♔xa5	♔c5
52	♔a4	b5+

53	♔b3	a5
	White resigns	

This was Michael's first success in competitive play against a 200+ graded opponent and he repeated the process three weeks later when he beat Peter Clarke and went on to win the Cornwall Lightning Championship for the first of six successive occasions.

In this season, we enjoyed a second family holiday at Torquay as the West of England Championships were held there and Michael was allowed to play, although we were told initially that his grade was too low. However when I pointed out that the grade was over six months old and that he had improved considerably since then, he was allowed to take part. He justified his appearance as the youngest ever player ever to play in the Championship section by finishing with three and a half points out of seven, only losing to Alan Ashby and Gerald Moore, who were to become regular opponents at west country events over the next few years.

Game 20   31.3.83
Adams-P.J.Meade
West of England Championship
Round Two
Sicilian Defence

1	e4	c5
2	♘f3	♘c6
3	c3	

Nowadays I am happy to go into the mainline of the Sicilian, but then I still treated 2 ... ♘c6 as a special case and transposed into a c3 Sicilian.

3	...	d5
4	exd5	♕xd5
5	d4	e6
6	♗e2	♘f6
7	0-0	♗e7

8	♗e3	cxd4
9	♘xd4	♘xd4
10	♗xd4	0-0
11	♘d2	e5

I have obtained the more pleasant game from the opening, so 11 ... e5 is extremely ambitious and out of keeping with the demands of Black's position. 11 ... ♗d7 12 ♗f3 ♕b5 would have been better.

12	♗f3	♕e6

If now 12 ... ♕b5 then 13 c4 maintains an edge. The move played results in an unfortunate pin from Black's point of view.

13	♖e1	♗d6
14	♕c2	♖e8

15	♖ad1	♛f5
16	♘e4!	

Without this move, Black's difficulties may have been resolved, but, due to tactics along the e-file, 16 ... exd4 is impossible because of 17 ♘xf6+, followed by 18 ♖xe8+. After 16 ♘e4, Black's difficulties are actually compounded.

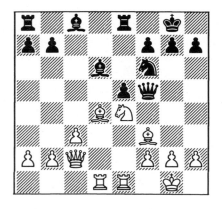

16	...	♗c7
17	♗c5	♘d7

Black's position would remain very difficult after 17 ... ♘xe4 18 ♗xe4, as his queenside is under great pressure from both white bishops and in order to complete his development, he will probably have to shed a pawn.

18	♛a4	a6
19	♘d6	

This gives me two bishops, to add to my other advantages.

19	...	♗xd6
20	♗xd6	h5
21	♗e4	♛f6
22	♛c4	♘f8
23	♗xf8	

White gives up one of his bishops in order to invade Black's position.

23	...	♖xf8
24	♛c7	g6
25	♖d6	♛g5
26	h4	♛g4
27	♖f6	

Although Black has not yet lost material, his position has further deteriorated as he has not yet developed his bishop on c8. Now his king's wing is in danger and his pieces are not occupying good defensive squares. His next move smacks of desperation.

27	...	♗f5
28	♗xf5	gxf5
29	♖xe5	♖ad8
30	♖d6	♖de8
31	♖d3	♛f4
32	♖de3	♖xe5
33	♛xe5	♛xe5
34	♖xe5	f4
35	♖g5+	♔h7
36	♖xh5+	♔g6
37	♖d5	♖e8
38	♔f1	♖e7
39	f3	♖e6
40	♔f2	b5
41	a3	f6
42	♔f1	**Resigns**

Resignation came at the adjournment, when my opponent decided that resumption was unnecessary.

This was my first ever win in the West of England Championships.

Michael enjoyed his first success for Cornwall in the quarter finals of the Minor Counties Championships against Buckinghamshire at Taunton. It had taken a long time coming and it was his eighth appearance for Cornwall. However as he improved, he was promoted to higher boards and his opponent's strength increased. Five of the games had been drawn but now he achieved his first success against K.Beedle (BCF 181), many others followed.

The British Championships were held at Southport. Now that Michael had won the Under 11 event, there seemed no point in playing in it again, so he entered a very strong Under 14 competition. We knew that it would provide a very strong test and were not really sure what would constitute a good result. It was a two week event over eleven rounds, which was longer than anything Michael had played in hitherto. It was the extra rounds that turned out to be Michael's undoing, although he had enjoyed a great run earlier.

Philip Rossiter and Michael dominated the event and they met as co-leaders in Round Six, having dropped only half a point. Up to then, Philip enjoyed a hundred per cent record in their four games, so it was a big psychological boost when Michael survived a very difficult adjournment session, with rook, knight and bishop holding off Philip's queen and extra pawns. Three straight wins followed to send Michael into a half point lead going into Round Ten, only for Philip to catch him after Michael took a cautious draw against Darren Wheeler. Early on in the final round, Michael was offered a draw by Ben Beake, but he declined the offer as Philip was still playing and went on to be defeated decisively. This left Philip requiring only a draw to take the title and this was duly achieved. Michael was bitterly disappointed to finish in second position with eight and a half points but at the beginning of the fortnight, we would gladly have settled for such a score against good players from older age groups.

Michael's performance did earn an invitation to play in the Lloyds Bank Masters, but we knew that he was not ready for that sort of event yet. Perhaps next year, we said.

6   On the Way to a Rating

It is a strange fact that Michael never won an Under Fourteen competition in his career. He often came close, but as at Southport something always went wrong. It did again in the Lloyds Bank Junior Under 14 Quickplay at the beginning of the new season. It started so well, as he won his first six games in a ten round event to enjoy a clear lead. Then he had a chance of revenge against Ben Beake and again came off second best. Worse still, he conceded another defeat and a draw in the last three rounds and had to be content with another second place.

As we passed time waiting for the prizegiving, I wandered along to the master scoreboard and as I was looking up various player's scores, contemplating what might have been, two people came up behind me and started talking about Michael. They were saying that Michael would never go very far in chess, because unlike his claim in "Play Chess", he failed to learn anything from his defeat against Ben Beake at Southport. Fortunately I had always kept a low profile at chess events so the speakers were not aware who the person standing in front of them was and I moved away. It is not always easy being the parent of a gifted child, as there are so many people eager to give advice and express opinions. As I was not at all sure what lay ahead of Michael, it was quite easy for me not to sing the praises of my own child. On the other hand, it did annoy me to hear this sort of criticism, but I would not have dreamed of responding. However I must admit that I would not mind meeting them now and reminding them of their predictions!

Anyway, Michael was growing up and had now moved on to secondary education at Truro School, which possessed a strong academic reputation as well as being a chess playing school. As Margaret had returned to full-time teaching at another school in Truro, we moved to the city to live. It was easier for me to drive to Falmouth each day, especially as Michael has never enjoyed a reputation as an early riser, at least not since he reached double figures.

Truro School, led by one Mark Crouse, had just achieved promotion to the Cornish First Division, so Michael continued to play the same opponents as he took over the top board spot. Michael led the team to several league and cup triumphs over the next few seasons with a very high success rate on top board. I suppose several outsiders would have argued that he was wasting his time playing in these games but no one in Cornwall thought so. His opponents enjoyed playing him even if they sometimes got tired of losing results. As for Michael, he enjoyed representing the school, as well as being with his friends. In this season, he won fifteen games, drew one and lost one, although the loss was due to trying to win a drawn ending for the team's needs and losing it.

Another good reason for continuing to play locally was the amount of genuine interest that Michael's chess achievements created among people, who had no previous interest in the game. Although they did not always play the game themselves, they became keenly interested in following Michael's career and also the exploits of other Cornish youngsters. It certainly encouraged us to know that so much support existed and we were very grateful for it.

His second season in Opens was much easier going and there was no doubt how much he benefited from the trials and tribulations of the previous season, although the learning process continued. His results were much improved and throughout a season of 125 graded games, Michael only lost seventeen, of which eleven were against players with grades in excess of 200. Incidentally Michael's grade for this season was 172.

Michael's second appearance in the Lloyds Bank Plymouth Junior International coincided with the first home success in the event, with English juniors filling the first three places. Philip Rossiter won the event, with David Norwood as runner-up and Michael in third spot. Michael won four games, drew the same number and lost to his long standing adversary.

Game 21	5.1.84	2 ♘c3	d5
P.Rossiter (BCF 193)-Adams		3 ♕f3	dxe4
Lloyds Bank Junior International		4 ♘xe4	♘d7

Round Five
Caro Kann Defence

1   e4   c6

Against this slightly unusual method of meeting the Caro-Kann, it is better to play 4 ... ♘f6 when the queen is misplaced on f3.

5	d4	♘gf6
6	♗c4	e6
7	♗g5	♗e7
8	h4	♘xe4
9	♕xe4	♘f6
10	♗xf6	♗xf6
11	♘f3	♕e7
12	0-0-0	♗d7
13	♘e5	0-0-0
14	♖h3!	

After this move, White's rook is well placed to swing over to the d-file or the queenside, whenever appropriate.

| 14 | ... | ♗xe5? |

Although I had a cramped and uncomfortable position, the problems would not have been too serious if I had continued with a move such as 14 ... ♔b8.

| 15 | dxe5 | c5 |

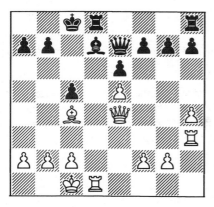

16   ♖d6

I overlooked this move, thinking that I would have time to play ... ♗c6, when Black's position would be fine.

| 16 | ... | ♗e8 |

16 ... f5 had to be tried, although my position was horrendous.

17	♖b3	♖d7
18	♗a6	♖c7
19	♗xb7+	♖xb7
20	♖d8+	♔xd8
21	♖xb7	♗d7
22	♖xa7	♕e8
23	♕d3	f6
24	♕d6	Resigns

I was disappointed with this defeat as with the one I had suffered at the hands of Ben Beake at Southport. Having ended the run of defeats at Philip's hands and knowing that a good performance in this tournament might influence the selection for the World Under 16 competition, I was quite determined to do well, especially as the tournament position was such that a win would allow me to overtake Philip and go into an outright lead. However a series of second best decisions in the opening and one very bad miscalculation meant that I was unable to put up serious resistance against his overwhelming attack. Philip went on to win the tournament and earn selection for the World Under 16 event.

A defeat like that should have left some mark on Michael, but in their next encounter he managed to achieve his first success against Philip. It had taken a long time coming, but felt all the better for that. For good measure, it won the best game prize at the West of England Championship.

Game 22   19.4.84
P.Rossiter (BCF 193)-Adams
West of England Championship
Round Two
Caro Kann Defence

1	e4	c6
2	d4	d5
3	exd5	cxd5
4	c4	♘f6
5	♘c3	g6
6	cxd5	♗g7
7	♕b3	0-0
8	♘f3	

My system is slightly frowned on in theoretical circles, but against it the most suitable place for the knight is not f3. More normal continuations are 8 ♗g5, 8 ♗e2 with the idea of ♗f3, and 8 g3, all aiming to protect the extra pawn on d5. To this end, White's knight will often head for f4 via e2, rather than to f3.

8	...	♘bd7
9	d6	

Realising he cannot hold the pawn, my opponent ensures that my d-pawn also becomes isolated.

9	...	exd6
10	♗f4	♘b6

11	♗e2	♗e6
12	♕d1	♘bd5
13	♘xd5	♘xd5
14	♗g3	♕a5+
15	♘d2	

The tempi that White has lost through the queen moves are important and this check presents a difficult situation. After 15 ♕d2 ♕xd2+ 16 ♔xd2 ♗h6+, I have also an advantage.

15	...	♗xd4
16	0-0	♘e3
17	♘b3	♘xd1
18	♘xa5	♘xb2
19	♗xd6	♖fc8
20	♗f3	♘c4
21	♖ad1	♘xa5
22	♖xd4	♖d8

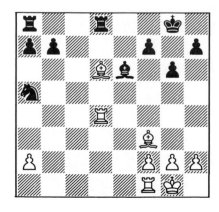

Thanks to some clever tactical play, my opponent, who was in desperate trouble earlier, has created an ending where I have considerable technical problems to overcome.

23	a4	♖ac8
24	h3	♘c4
25	♖c1	♘xd6
26	♖cd1	♔f8
17	♖xd6	♖xd6
28	♖xd6	♔e7
29	♖d4	b6
30	♗e2	♖c1+
31	♔h2	♖c2
32	♖e4	♔d6
33	♔g3	♗d5
34	♖e3	♖b2
35	f3	h5
36	♗f1	♖a2
37	♗b5	h4+
38	♔xh4	♖xg2
39	f4	f6
40	♖d3	♔c5
41	♗a6	♗f7
42	♖g3	♖xg3

43	♔xg3	♗e6?

This move lost time and 43 ... ♔d4 was better.

44	♗d3	♗f7
45	h4	♔b4?

My sealed move, before the adjournment. Again 45 ... ♔d4 was better.

46	♗c2?	

46 ♗b5 was better. The move played allowed me to correct the error on the sealed move, although I was winning in any case.

46	...	♔c3
47	♗e4	♔d4
48	♗c2	f5
49	h5	gxh5
50	♔h4	♔e3
51	♔g5	♗e6
52	♔f6	♗c8
53	♔e5	h4
54	♗b3	♗b7

White resigns

Michael illustrated his improvement by increasing his score from three and a half to five points and this was good enough to earn him third place behind Gary Lane and David Lemoir. Michael's only defeat was at the hands of Gary and his four wins and two draws helped him to a tournament grading of 215, which was the best of his career up to that point.

If there had been any doubt whether Michael had become the youngest ever county champion the previous season, there was certainly none this year as he won the Emigrant Cup with four wins and a draw in the final round.

His performance in the British Lightning event raised more eyebrows when he finished in third position behind Mark Hebden and Jonathan Levitt. Michael would have done even better if he had not been swindled by Mark to lose an ending that should have been drawn. Mark was to take over the role of bogeyman to Michael for the next few years. Whenever they played in the same tournament, Michael and Mark were frequently paired and Michael always came off second best.

Further publicity came Michael's way, when a simultaneous exhibition was given by Gary Kasparov, then the rising star, as one of the sideshows at the USSR against the Rest of the World match. Five English juniors faced Kasparov "over the board" in the London Docklands, while five Americans played by satellite link-up. Kasparov won seven of his games and conceded draws to Gary Lane, Neil Carr and Michael. The press and television seized on Michael's result and largely ignored the achievements of Gary and Neil. Michael travelled in VIP style in a courtesy car with Kasparov and Russian officials to make another television appearance. He did say that the Russians were very pleasant to him and spoke to him in English.

Game 23   5.7.84
G.Kasparov-Adams
Satellite Simultaneous
Caro-Kann Defence

1	e4	c6
2	d4	d5
3	♘d2	dxe4
4	♘xe4	♘d7
5	♘f3	

5 ♘g5, which Kasparov has also used, is currently the sternest theoretical test of this variation.

5	...	♘gf6
6	♘g3	e6
7	♗d3	♗e7
8	0-0	0-0
9	c3	c5
10	♕e2	b6

11	♗f4	♗b7
12	♖ad1	cxd4
13	♘xd4	♘d5
14	♗c1	♕c7
15	♗b1	♘7f6
16	♘h5	g6
17	♘xf6+	♘xf6
18	♖fe1	♖fe8
19	♗g5	♘d5
20	♗xe7	½-½

An unremarkable draw, if it had not been played against the rising star of world chess. Kasparov offered the draw, presumably because it was going to be difficult to make any headway and it would enable him to spend more time on the remaining nine games, as the simultaneous was being played with clocks.

Encouraged by the good results throughout the season, we decided that Michael should enter the Major Open at the BCF Championships at Brighton. It was not an easy decision to make. Looking back, we were attracted by the large injection of prize-money into the Major Open, while there was always the hope, no matter how remote, of qualifying for the following year's British Championships. On the other hand, even if he won the Under 14 event, it would not have benefited him very much in terms of improving his play and any other result would have been regarded as a failure. Nevertheless it was with some reluctance that we made our choice.

A first round defeat by Brian Denman, who was a 200+ player, ensured that Michael was always struggling around the half way mark in a very strong field. He was in very good company, but it was not the sort of result we had hoped for. His best win was against Gavin Crawley (BCF 212), but overall his tournament grade was only 187. On the long drive back to Cornwall, we kept on trying to convince ourselves that we had made the right decision, saying that the experience would stand him in good stead in the future.

Besides, there were two more tournaments before the end of the season. First, there was the Lloyds Bank Junior Squad age group quickplays. Being consistent, we chose the Under 21 event and Michael responded by finishing in sixth position, losing only to Karl Bowden among ten opponents and drawing with Stuart Conquest and Joe Gallagher.

On the next day, he had the privilege of playing Boris Spassky, former world champion, in a curtain raiser to the Lloyds Bank Masters event. Both players were allowed seven minutes for all their moves.

Game 24   22.3.84
B.Spassky-Adams
Lloyds Bank Masters
Curtain-Raiser
Caro Kann Defence

1	e4	c6
2	d4	d5
3	e5	♗f5
4	h4	h5

5	c4	e6
6	♘c3	♘d7
7	♗g5	♗e7
8	♕d2	dxc4

Up to now, the moves have followed my game against Gary Lane (Game 19), but my eighth sought an improvement.

9	♗xc4	♘b6

10	♗b3	♗xg5?!

Generally it is not desirable for Black to swap these bishops, although it helped me to complete my development. Possibly 10 ... ♘h6 was stronger.

11	hxg5	♘e7
12	♘f3	♘bd5
13	♘h4	g6
14	0-0	0-0
15	♖ad1	♕c7
16	♖fe1	♖ad8
17	♘a4	♔g7
18	f3	b6
19	♖c1	♕b7
20	♔h2	c5

After a spell of manoeuvring, I reluctantly decided to break open the game. Although it is objectively to White's advantage, I was worried about White preparing g4 and trapping my bishop on f5.

21	dxc5	b5

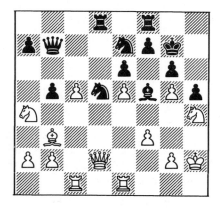

22	c6!	

This will enable the white knight to reach a powerful post on c5.

22	...	♘xc6
23	♘c5	♕b6
24	♕f2	♘f4
25	♕e3	♘d5

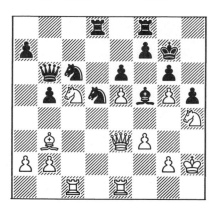

26	♘xe6+	

This combination contained the right ingredients, but was executed in the wrong order. Better was 26 ♘xf5+ first.

26	...	♗xe6
27	♕xb6	♘xb6
28	♗xe6	♘b4
29	♗b3	

This is a mistake. After 29 ♖c7 White would hold a big advantage.

29	...	♘d3
30	e6	

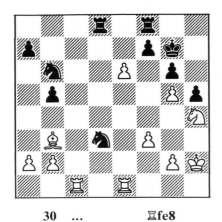

30   ...   ♖fe8

Much safer was 30 ... ♘xc1,
with the idea of 31 e7 ♘xb3,
giving an ending which is slightly
better for Black. My move was

too ambitious, possibly due to the
shortage of time. My opponent
had about three minutes left and I
had a few seconds.

31	♖c7	♘xe1
32	♖xf7+	♔g8
33	♘xg6	♘c4
34	♘e7+	♔h8

Better was 34 ... ♖xe7, although
the avalanche of white pawns
would make the position difficult
to defend.

| 35 | g6 | ♖xe7 |
| 36 | ♖xe7 | **Resigns** |

Technically I lost on time, but
my knights are far too slow moving
to cope with the pawns anyway.

We decided that Michael should compete in the Masters event for the
first time. Having just played a former world champion, we expected
Michael to slip back to anonymity among the middle boards, while he
continued the learning process, as at Brighton. However chess is not
predictable and Michael went on to reach heights that I had never
contemplated even in my wildest dreams.

He started with a win against D.Sedgwick (BCF 178) and then played
eight rated players. For the benefit of non-chess players, I should point
out that gradings are used for national purposes but ratings are
international. While any registered player, regardless of standard, can be
given a grade, only those with a standard in excess of a BCF 200 grade are
rated on the basis of their results against other rated players. To gain a
rating initially, players have to perform above this level for a minimum of
nine games.

A grade of 200 is equivalent to a rating of 2200, one of 220 to 2360, one
of 240 to 2520 and so on. As Michael's grade was 172 at the beginning of
the season, he had no right to draw with R.Seppeur (FIDE 2310) and then
beat Neil Dickenson (FIDE 2230). This earned him a game with Mark
Hebden (FIDE 2480), which was inevitably lost, but Michael bounced

back to defeat M.Pasman (FIDE 2310), an Israeli Federation Master, and followed that with draws against IM Elect Jonathan Levitt (FIDE 2370) and International Master Michael Wilder (FIDE 2460) from the USA. He did lose in Round Eight against International Master Greenfeld (FIDE 2485) of Israel, but only after an adjournment session, for which he was prepared by several senior English players. Finally in the final round came the best result of all, his first competitive success against an International Master, Saeed Ahmed (FIDE 2430), from the United Arab Emirates.

Game 25	30.8.84

Adams-Saeed Ahmed (FIDE 2430)
Lloyds Bank Masters
Round Nine
Sicilian Defence

1	e4	c5
2	♘f3	♘c6
3	d4	cxd4
4	♘xd4	♘f6
5	♘c3	d6
6	♗e3	♘g4
7	♗g5	♕b6

Better was 7 ... h6 8 ♗h4 g5 9 ♗g3 ♗g7, with unclear play.

8	♗b5	♗d7
9	0-0	♕xd4
10	♗xc6	♕xd1
11	♗xd7+	♔xd7
12	♖axd1	

Many commentators consider this ending to be equal, but I believe that White's superior development and the position of Black's king leave White with an edge.

12	...	g6

13	h3	♘e5
14	♘d5	♘c6
15	b4	h6
16	♗h4	f5
17	f4	♖g8
18	b5	♘a5
19	e5	♘c4
20	♖d4	♖c8

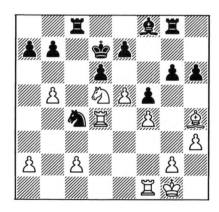

21 e6+!

My play was aggressive and I have taken risks by pushing forward my b-pawn. However the activity of my pieces justified this decision. If now, 21 ... ♔xe6 22 ♖e1+

causes a huge accident on the e7 square.

21	...	♔e8
22	b6!	

If Black is given time to consolidate, he may be able to pick off the weak white pawns. By forcing open the queenside, with little regard for material, I can take advantage of Black's undeveloped forces. The reply is forced as I am threatening 23 ♘c7+.

22	...	axb6
23	♖b1	g5
24	♖b4	b5
25	♖xb5	

If now 25 ... gxh4 26 ♖xb7 ♘a5 27 ♖d7, the idea of ♘c7+ is still strong for me.

25	...	♗g7
26	♖xc4!	

The final sacrifice makes the rest of the game simple. My opponent is unable to resist my powerfully placed pieces and resignation looms.

26	...	♖xc4
27	♖xb7	♗d4+
28	♗f2	♗xf2+
29	♔xf2	♔f8
30	♖xe7	♖g7
31	♖d7	♖xc2+
32	♔f3	♖g6
33	♖d8+	♔g7
34	e7	g4+
35	hxg4	fxg4+
36	♔g3	**Resigns**

Frantic mathematical calculations revealed that he had missed an International Master norm by the narrowest of margins, but as we had not even considered the possibility, there was no disappointment. Various calculations revealed a tournament performance of somewhere between 2385 and 2420, depending on whose mathematics you believed. However Michael could not be awarded a rating as he had only played eight rated opponents. Nevertheless it was virtually certain that participation in one more suitable event would guarantee him an international rating. That would confirm his transition from a promising junior to someone who could hold their own with top players.

I had become used to Michael achieving better results than I had anticipated, but without doubt this was the greatest surprise so far. What was most encouraging was that he had maintained good form over nine rounds against international players. We were looking forward to next season already.

7 British Championship Debut

Michael's new grade of 192 indicated that he was about the two hundredth best player in Britain, as there were about that number with higher grades. However if Michael could clinch his rating, then he would leapfrog past most of them and certainly reach the top forty. Thus the gaining of a rating became important.

He was extremely fortunate that there were others in a similar position and the Chequers Rating Tournament was arranged and happened to coincide with Michael's half-term. At this stage, there was no intention that he would become a full-time chess player and generally chess took second place behind school. I did keep an eye on those who were trying to make a living out of chess and the success rate appeared to be quite low. Consequently it was very rare for Michael to take time off school at this time. In a contemporary newspaper article, I notice that Michael was quoted as saying, "I don't think I will ever earn my living from chess – I think I'll have a job and play chess in my spare time."

Some reaction to the Lloyds Bank Masters result was expected and a fall from the initial calculations was anticipated but instead Michael went through the tournament unbeaten to finish in second place with four wins and five draws. The four most significant results were against the rated opponents – two wins against Joe Gallagher (FIDE 2295) and Andrew Muir (FIDE 2255) and two draws against D.Savereide (FIDE 2230) and Gavin Crawley (FIDE 2300), the tournament winner.

Game 26 27.10.84		2 ♘f3	d6
Adams-D.Agnos (BCF 207)		3 d4	cxd4
Chequers Rating Tournament		4 ♘xd4	♘f6
Round Seven		5 ♘c3	a6
Sicilian Defence		6 ♗g5	e6
		7 f4	♗e7
1 e4	c5	8 ♕f3	♕c7

9	0-0-0	♘bd7
10	g4	b5
11	♗xf6	♘xf6
12	g5	♘d7
13	f5	♘c5
14	f6	gxf6
15	gxf6	♗f8
16	a3	

This is a well known line, but 16 a3 is not critical. More common at the time was 16 ♕h5, although recent research has centred around 16 ♖g1, with the idea of sacrificing the exchange with a later ♖g7.

16	...	♖b8

A more usual plan for Black, and certainly a safer one, is to continue 16 ... ♗d7, with the idea of 0-0-0.

17	♖e1	♗d7
18	♗h3	a5

This move shows little awareness of the dangers that Black is facing. By committing his queen's rook so early, his king becomes stuck in the centre, which is extremely dangerous. Perhaps 18 ... ♔d8 was better.

(see diagram)

19 ♘d5!

After 19 ... exd5 20 exd5+ ♔d8 21 ♗xd7 ♕xd7 22 ♘c6+ ♔c7 23 ♘xb8 ♔xb8, although Black

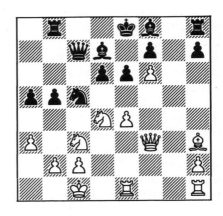

would hold a nominal material advantage, the lack of mobility available to his pieces and the dangerous position of his king would mean that White would stand better. Despite this, it was much superior to the game move, which gave me an extremely powerful attack.

19	...	♕b7
20	♕h5	♖c8
21	♔b1	b4
22	a4	♖g8?

By attempting to play on the kingside, Black only hastens the end. Better was 22 ... ♘xa4, with the idea of ... ♘c3+.

23	♕xh7	♖g6
24	♖hg1	♖xg1
25	♖xg1	exd5
26	♖g8	Resigns

After 26 ... ♗xh3 27 ♖xf8+ wins.

Calculating a rating is something that I have never understood, so when I read in the papers that it was likely to be in the region of 2400 and that this figure put him in the category of child prodigies like Bobby Fischer, Mecking and Nigel Short, I assumed it to be true. In the event an administrative misunderstanding meant that Michael's name did not appear on the January list and when the rating was eventually published on the July list, it was 2360. However we were not too concerned about the reduction as 2360 was the rating that secured automatic qualification for the British Championship in Edinburgh.

However that was a long way off when the Chequers event was completed. It was back to school and local tournaments for the next six months. I sometimes wonder what would have happened if Michael had been brought up in London. As Margaret and I had spent the first three years of our married life living in London, I suppose it could have happened. Little did I know that when we moved back to our native Cornwall that we were going to produce a son that would involve return trips to London at such frequent intervals. It is impossible to assess how well Michael would have done had he lived in London, but to have had frequent access to strong tournaments and good coaching would certainly have been beneficial. On the other hand, it is possible that he might have suffered from having too much chess and lacked some of the enthusiasm for London events that he displayed because of their rarity value. My firm belief is that living in Cornwall helped, rather than hindered, his career, but it can never be proved.

Michael's next tournament after Chequers was the Cornwall Under 13 event. It is difficult for outsiders to appreciate that he enjoyed being with his contemporaries at such events. In any case, his fifth successive triumph was only achieved on tie-break from Mathew Piper.

Although I have lamented the lack of a very strong player in the area, Michael was very fortunate that he always had friends, who could give him a good game. Initially it had been Mark Crouse and now it was Mathew, a classmate of Michael's. I am not sure how many games of chess that they played during school lunchtimes but it must have run into several hundred. It helped Michael a lot and Mathew went on to achieve some very good results. I have commented how Michael helped the King Charles boys and he was always prepared to help those who sought help, but would never impose himself on others. This was also apparent at Truro School and some of the team's success was due to preparation with Michael before games.

Michael enjoyed his first success in the Torbay Open, albeit as part of a quintuple tie. He did have the opportunity of winning it outright but settled for a three move draw in the last round. It is easy to criticise such caution and several did, but the prospect of a thirteen year old knowing that a draw will confirm the winning of a minimum prize of £80, while a defeat would result in failure to make the prize list, makes it difficult to alter and I felt it was fair enough.

Another Open that Michael played in regularly was the Cotswold event, that was held at Stroud, before moving to Gloucester. It always coincides with the schools' summer half-term. Michael did not win the event this year, as he lost to Chris Beaumont, but his four and a half points out of six was the equivalent of a 209 grading performance.

Game 27   26.5.85
D.Osborne (BCF 193)-Adams
Cotswold Open, Round Four
Caro-Kann Defence

1	e4		c6
2	d4		d5
3	e5		♗f5
4	h4		h5
5	♘e2		e6
6	♘g3		♗g6
7	♗e2		

This particular idea in the advance variation of the Caro-Kann Defence does not enjoy a particularly good reputation. Black should be able to equalise without difficulty.

7	...		c5
8	c3		♘c6
9	♗e3		♘ge7
10	a3		

This is an idea more common in the French Defence. The dif-ference between its adoption there and here is that Black's light square bishop already occupies a good post whereas in the French Defence, it is often restricted inside the pawn chain.

10	...		c4
11	♗xh5		

Although this pawn grab may justify the development of White's pieces, it is not sound here. A better plan was 11 ♘d2, possibly followed by b3.

11	...		♗xh5
12	♘xh5		♘f5
13	g3		♕b6
14	♗c1		0-0-0

Even stronger was 14 ... ♘fxd4 15 cxd4 ♕xd4, with threats of ... ♕e4+ and ... ♕xd1, followed by ... ♖xh5.

15	♖f1		♔b8
16	♘d2		

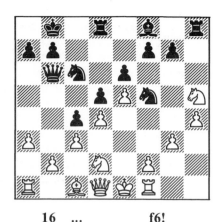

16 ... f6!

Due to the exposed nature of White's king, it is in Black's interest to break open the centre immediately, without great concern for the amount of material lost – so long as it is compensated by open lines towards White's king.

| 17 | exf6 | gxf6 |
| 18 | b3 | e5 |

Continuing the strategy started with 16 ... f6 and leaving White's king hopelessly exposed.

19	♘xf6	exd4
20	bxc4	♗g7
21	♕f3	♗xf6
22	♕xf5	♖he8+
23	♔d1	dxc3
24	♕xf6	c2+

White resigns

This wins White's queen, after 24 ♔xc2 ♘b4+ 25 axb4 ♕xf6. Perhaps I am better known as a positional player, but this performance shows that, in the right circumstances, I can also attack.

He continued his improvement in the West of England Championships and moved up to the runner-up slot. Gary Lane was the winner for the fourth successive time, beating Michael decisively in their third round clash. Four wins and two draws in his other games gave him a 214 grading performance.

Game 28   8.4.85
Adams-G.Burgess (BCF 170)
West of England Championship
Round Seven
Sicilian Defence

1	e4	c5
2	♘f3	e6
3	d4	cxd4
4	♘xd4	♘f6
5	♘c3	d6
6	♗e2	♘c6
7	0-0	♗e7
8	♗e3	♗d7
9	♔h1	

Better here was 9 f4. The move played gives Black an early chance to equalise.

| 9 | ... | ♘xd4 |
| 10 | ♗xd4 | |

Another inaccuracy. 10 ♕xd4 would have been slightly stronger.

10	...	♗c6
11	♗d3	e5
12	♗e3	d5
13	exd5	♘xd5
14	♘xd5	♕xd5
15	f3	0-0
16	♗e4	♕xd1

Not the best. 16 ... ♕e6 would have left the game equal. In this ending, White's queenside majority gives me an advantage.

17	♖axd1	♗xe4
18	fxe4	♖fd8
19	c4	b6
20	g4	♖ac8
21	b3	f6
22	♖d5	♔f7
23	♔g2	♔e6
24	♖fd1	g6

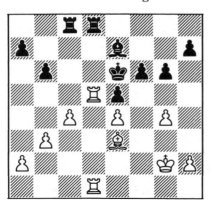

25 a4!

This move threatens to decimate the black queenside by a5. As the bishop is tied to the defence of the rook on d8, Black is forced to make some kind of concession.

25	...	f5
26	♔f3	♖xd5
27	exd5+	♔d6
28	gxf5	gxf5
29	a5	bxa5?

A bad error. He should have played 29 ... ♗d8 to defend the b-pawn. The move played gives White two passed pawns, well supported by the rook and bishop. In contrast, Black's passed pawns are going nowhere.

| 30 | ♗xa7 | a4 |

Better was 30 ... ♔d7, halting the immediate advance of the white pawns.

31	c5+	♔d7
32	c6+	♔c7
33	bxa4	♖a8
34	♗f2	♖xa4
35	♖b1	♖b4
36	♖a1	♔d6
37	♖a7	e4+

Fortunately for me, in the variation 37 ... ♔xd5 38 ♖xe7 ♔xc6 39 ♖xe5, the rook's pawn has the correct colour queening square, thus making the technical process relatively simple.

38	♔f4	e3+
39	♔xe3	♗g5+
40	♔d3	♔xd5

41	c7	**Resigns**

After 41 ... ♖c4 42 ♖a5+ wins the rook.

A disappointment was experienced in the Lloyds Bank Plymouth Junior International. It started well enough as Michael recorded three straight wins, but his inability to beat his English compatriots, Dimitrios Agnos and Neil McDonald, and a defeat against the West German, S.Maus, put him out of the running.

By this time Michael had earned top board spot in the Cornwall team and was winning fairly regularly, although the team continued to struggle. However by defeating Dorset, they did qualify for the final rounds of the Minor Counties event, where they were defeated by Surrey.

Game 29   13.4.85
H.Barber (BCF 209)-Adams
Cornwall v. Surrey
Minor Counties Quarter-Final
Caro Kann Defence

1	e4	c6
2	d4	d5
3	exd5	cxd5
4	c4	♘f6
5	c5	

This opening variation is not particularly dangerous for Black, as the tension in the centre is released too quickly. More usual is 5 ♘c3.

5	...	g6!

The best reply. 5 ... e6 gives more justification to the early queenside push by White.

6	♘c3	♗g7

7	♗b5+	♗d7
8	♗xd7+	♕xd7
9	♘f3	♘c6
10	0-0	0-0
11	♖b1	♘e4

White has played the opening without inspiration and Black already stands better.

12	♗e3	f5

However I should have given more thought to a move like 12 ... b6 to combat the danger posed by White's queenside majority.

13	♘e2	a5
14	b3	e6

14 ... b6, with the idea of 15 cxb6 ♖ab8 was a more positional way to play. My move was more interesting and more dangerous.

15	a3	♗f6

16	b4	axb4
17	axb4	g5
18	b5	♞a5
19	♞e5	♛g7
20	f4	♝xe5
21	dxe5	♞c4
22	♛d4	

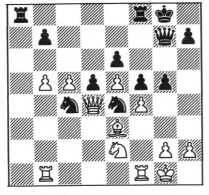

22 ...   ♜a2

With Black's knights occupying such dominant posts, it is strange that Black does not have a more clear-cut continuation. 22 ... ♜a3 forcing 23 ♝c1 ♜a2 would have succeeded in forcing White's bishop to a less effective post.

23	♞g3	♞xg3
24	hxg3	♜fa8
25	♜f2	♜2a3
26	♜e2	♜8a4

27	c6	♞xe3
28	♜xe3	♜xd4
29	♜xa3	♛c7
30	♜a8+	♚f7
31	♚h2	

My opponent probably planned to continue 31 ♜a7, but I can play 31 ... ♜d1+ 32 ♜xd1 ♛b6+, winning easily. Whilst the technical conversion happened fairly quickly, it is worth noting that if his king was on a different square in this variation, he might not even be losing.

31	...	gxf4
32	♜a7	fxg3+
33	♚h3	♚g6
34	♜xb7	♛d8
35	♚xg3	♛h4+
36	♚f3	♛f4+

White resigns

I was somewhat short-sighted in this game, becoming so over-excited with my kingside prospects that I did not take proper steps to eliminate the dangers posed by White's queenside pawns. If I had done so, my positional advantages should have told and there would have been less risk for me. Still I was only thirteen and playing on top board.

Michael played in the Under 18 section of the Lloyds Bank BCF Squad event and won the event on tie break, despite faltering in the last two rounds. After beating J.Nelson (BCF 170), Jeremy Sharp (BCF 185),

Aaron Summerscale (BCF 186) and David Wood (BCF 185), he lost to J.Goddard (BCF 181) and drew with Philip Morris (BCF 185). Generally it was a pleasing result bearing in mind that Michael was still an Under 13, although it would have been more preferable to have had a more clear-cut triumph.

Actually Michael travelled on his own to London for this event. It was getting more and more difficult for me to travel with him on every occasion. Besides it was good for Michael to be obtaining a degree of independence, although having said that we always arranged for him to be met at Paddington and fixed up where he was staying. Margaret and I will always be grateful to the many London and Home Counties players and families who looked after Michael during chess events and treated him like one of their own. There must have been fifteen or more who could claim "Michael slept here".

In the summer, he was selected to represent England in the Glorney Cup, which was some compensation for being passed over as England's representative in the World Under 16 for a second successive year. Philip Rossiter had been selected in 1984 and this time it was Dimitrios Agnos. At least, the Glorney selection showed that he had not been forgotten and ironically he was chosen on Board Three, two boards above Philip. The rest of the team was John Emms (1), David Watts (2), Mark Wheeler (4) and Chris Ward (6). The team won the event by three points from the host country, the Netherlands, and Michael won a best board prize for his undefeated record of four wins and a draw. This was the first occasion that he travelled overseas and he set the trend for nearly all his subsequent travel by failing to send any correspondence to his anxious parents. When his mum tackled him on the subject, he informed her that they did not appear to have letter boxes in Holland.

Shortly afterwards we were somewhat surprised and very pleased to read that Michael had come third in the Legal and General Player of the Year vote by chess journalists, behind John Nunn and Nigel Short. This recognition was most encouraging, although we realised that votes had been earned by youthful appeal rather than consistency of results at the highest level.

I was just as pleased when King Charles School Under Nine side won the National Primary Schools Team Championships. To this day, I am not sure how much I helped Michael with his chess and as I explained earlier, Michael must take most of the credit for the Under Eleven team's success in 1982. However it was my work that was responsible for this success and I felt that I had proved to myself that I had learned to teach chess. For good measure, the Under Eleven side also qualified for the National Finals for the first of three successive appearances.

Eventually the long awaited British Championships arrived. We hoped for a repeat performance of the sort of results that Michael had produced in the Lloyds Bank Masters, but had not forgotten the disappointment of the Major Open, which had preceded it.

For once, we did not go as a family. I think this was probably due to the fact that it was not a seaside venue, but in Edinburgh. I know that Margaret and Janet did not regret their decision to remain in Cornwall, as the weather in Scotland that summer was such that we were glad to have hot water bottles and electric blankets where we were staying, while the choice of a curling rink as the venue did nothing to raise the temperature.

Another factor may have been that Michael wanted to travel by rail via London so that he could play in the British Rail Quickplay event, which was held in two coaches of an intercity train, as it sped from King's Cross to Edinburgh. The players were allowed five minutes for all their moves and no rail journey can have passed so quickly for Michael. He won his group and qualified for a final all-play-all with Keith Arkell, Neil Carr, Stuart Conquest, Nigel Davies, Daniel King, Jonathan Levitt and Andrew Martin. When he emerged with the highest score from this group, we believed that he had won the event, but he was relegated to second place as he had dropped a point while qualifying for the final group and Stuart Conquest took first prize.

Michael appeared in the Championship as the second youngest player after Nigel Short to qualify. As his rating was so high, he had what looked a comparatively easy game against S.D.Singh (BCF 185) in the first round, but he had to settle for an uninspiring draw. He followed this with a defeat against R.Abayasekera (BCF 200), after pushing too hard for a win. Perhaps it's going to be another Major Open, we thought, but two wins and four draws followed to cheer us up. Michael lost to Colin McNab in Round Nine, but should have reached the fifty per cent mark in the next game.

Game 30 8.8.85		
D.Barua (FIDE 2410)-**Adams**		
British Championship, Round Ten		
Caro Kann Defence		
1	e4	c6
2	d4	d5
3	exd5	cxd5
4	♗d3	♘c6

5	c3	♘f6
6	h3	

This move is too passive to cause Black problems and 6 ♗f4 is more critical.

6	...	g6
7	♘f3	♗g7
8	0-0	0-0
9	♖e1	♕c7
10	♘bd2	♗f5
11	♘f1	

Barua's openings often look as if he is simply trying to reach the middle game rather than obtain an advantage from the opening. 11 ♗xf5 would have been a more critical test. Now Black is able to exchange the light squared bishops at no cost, with an easy game in prospect.

11	...	♗xd3
12	♕xd3	a6

It is standard procedure for Black to launch a minority attack in this kind of position, in order to create weaknesses on White's queenside. His move prepares ... b5 and ... b4.

13	♘g3	e6
14	♗g5	b5
15	♕d2	♖fc8
16	♗h6	♘a5
17	h4	

An overambitious move. 17 ♖ab1 was a necessary defensive resource.

17	...	♘c4
18	♕c1	♗xh6
19	♕xh6	♘xb2
20	♘e5	

White has lost a pawn for insufficient compensation. However I have few defenders around my king, so a white attack could still be dangerous.

20	...	♕d8
21	h5	♖a7
22	♖e3	♘c4
23	♘xc4	♖xc4
24	♖f3	

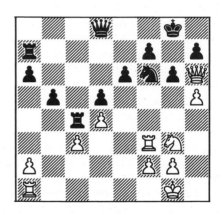

24	...	♘g4

A very strong manoeuvre, which expels White's queen. Although it creates some weaknesses, such as the pawn on e6, these should not be too serious. I simply have to convert my advantage into victory.

25	♕f4	f5
26	♕d2	

White was threatened by ... e5, as his d-pawn was pinned.

26	...	♖ac7
27	♖e1	♖7c6
28	♘f1	b4

Not the most accurate decision. I should have consolidated before taking any action, by playing 28 ... ♕f6.

29	cxb4	♖c2
30	♕d3	♕h4
31	g3	♕xh5
32	b5	♖c1?

After 32 ... axb5 33 ♕xb5 ♘e5, I was winning. Now the tables are turned.

| 33 | bxc6 | ♖xe1 |
| 34 | ♔g2 | ♖c1 |

(see diagram)

| 35 | ♕c3! | |

I missed this move and searched

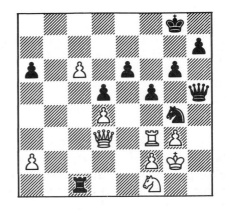

desperately for a defence that was not there.

35	...	♖xf1
36	♔xf1	♕h1+
37	♔e2	♘h2
38	c7	♕f1+
39	♔d2	♘xf3+
40	♕xf3	♕c4
41	♕c3	♕xa2+
42	♔e3	**Resigns**

A final round draw meant that he had finished with a disappointing final score of five out of eleven. However we were far from despondent and knew that Michael was capable of a much higher score than that. The immediate target would be to ensure that he qualified for next year's Championship, as his rating was beginning to slip.

8   International Master Norms

Michael began the new season with a grade of 208, which was less than the equivalent of his inflated rating, but was a more accurate indication of his playing strength as it was based on far more games. In any case, his rating was bound to drop on the January list because of his relatively poor results at Edinburgh. To reach the 200 mark seemed a significant step forward and his new grade placed him on the edge of the top eighty British players. When he had been younger, he had gone in awe of 200 grades and now he was one himself.

The season began at Paignton, where Michael had competed the previous season without conspicuous success, scoring four out of seven and finding the slow tempo of one game a day rather tedious. Usually Paignton coincided with the beginning of term in state schools and we were unable to accompany Michael, whose school always had longer holidays. However we must have returned to school later than usual and for some reason Margaret decided to travel with him, perhaps because I had been to Edinburgh. It turned out to be a unique and successful occasion, although it did not start like that as Michael was very sick during the first night and had to be nursed through the second and third days, when he drew his games. Once he had recovered, there was no chance of time weighing heavily on his hands as he was taken for walks, visits and swims, whenever he had a spare moment. It did his chess no harm and wins against P.C.Griffiths (BCF 218), P.W.Hempson (BCF 195) and A.Mordue (BCF 193), with a draw against Alan Ashby (BCF 208), ensured a share of first place with five and a half out of seven.

Game 31 4.9.85	1 e4	e5
Adams–P.C.Griffiths (BCF 218)	2 ♘f3	♘c6
Paignton, Round Four	3 ♗c4	♗c5
Evans Gambit	4 b4	♗xb4

5	c3	♗e7
6	d4	d6

Theory recommends 6 ... ♘a5 7 ♘xe5 ♘xc4 8 ♘xc4 d5 9 exd5 ♕xd5 10 ♘e3, with a slight edge for White.

7	♕b3	♘a5
8	♗xf7+	♔f8
9	♕a4	♔xf7
10	♕xa5	b6
11	♕b5	♗d7
12	♕e2	♗f6
13	0-0	♘e7
14	dxe5	dxe5

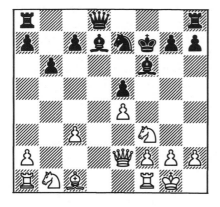

15   ♘xe5+

An over-optimistic move, although perhaps the one most in the spirit of the opening. 15 ♗g5 would have given White a safe edge.

15	...	♗xe5
16	♕h5+	♘g6
17	f4	♗f6

18	f5	♗c6
19	fxg6+	hxg6
20	♕e2	

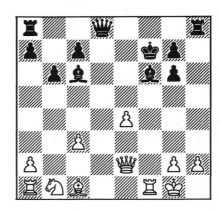

This position was not too promising. My first wave of attack has been beaten off and I have to spend time bringing up reinforcements. Black was far too obliging in giving me this time. He should have replied 20 ... ♕d6 21 e5 ♖ae8 22 ♗f4 (22 ♕c4+ ♗d5) ♕c5+, winning. White must play 21 ♗f4 ♕c5+ 22 ♗e3 but 22 ... ♗b5 and 22 ... ♕b5 both look good for Black.

20	...	♕d7
21	♗g5	

21 a4 (to stop ♗b5) ♖ae8 is hideous for White.

21	...	♖ae8?

Very strong, indeed decisive, at this stage would have been 21 ... ♗b5! 22 c4 ♕d4+.

22	♘d2	♖e5?

Better was 22 ... ♖h5, although by this stage White no longer stands worse.

23	♘f3	♖e7
24	♖ad1	♕e8
25	♕c4+	♔f8
26	e5!	

My attack has grown to enormous proportions very quickly as Black has never dealt with his exposed king position. A pleasing queen sacrifice concludes the game.

26	...	♗b5
27	exf6	♗xc4
28	fxe7+	♔f7

If 28 ... ♔g8 29 ♖d8 wins simply, but the move played does not prolong Black's resistance.

29	♘e5+	♔e6
30	♘xc4	♕b5
31	♖fe1+	**Resigns**

A month later, Michael returned to Devon for the Hexagon Open. It was an attempt to revive the successful events that had been held in Woolacombe, at the start of Michael's career, only this tournament was held at the Plymouth Guildhall. Unfortunately, the number of players was disappointing and only 24 competed in the Open, although the entry did include England's newest grandmaster, Jim Plaskett, and six others graded above 200. Michael defeated one of these, Angus Dunnington, in Round Two and then faced his first grandmaster in competition.

Game 32   5.10.85
J.Plaskett (BCF 243)-Adams
Hexagon Open, Round Three
Caro Kann Defence

1	e4	c6
2	d4	d5
3	e5	♗f5
4	c4	e6
5	♘c3	♘d7
6	♗e3	

This system is less dangerous than when the moves h4 ... h5 have been included, as in the games against Lane and Spassky.

6	...	♘e7
7	♘f3	dxc4
8	♗xc4	♘b6
9	♗d3	

More normal in this variation is 9 ♗b3 and to play the knight from g1 to e2. Plaskett tries a different configuration but the absence of light squared bishops can only be in Black's favour.

9	...	♗xd3
10	♕xd3	♘ed5

11	h4	♗e7
12	h5	h6
13	♖h3	

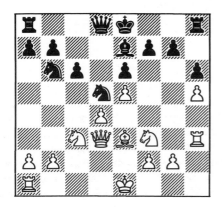

| 13 | ... | 0-0! |

A brave move. White's early pawn kingside advance could prove very dangerous. I did consider sacrificing some pawns on the kingside, playing ... ♕d7 and castling long, but the text move is much stronger as White's attack is not as powerful as it looks at first glance.

14	♖g3	♔h8
15	♔e2	

An immediate sacrifice such as 15 ♗xh6 gxh6 16 ♕d2 is refuted by 16 ... ♗g5, although the best that this sacrifice can achieve is a draw after 16 ... ♔h7 17 ♕d3+ ♔h8 and this was unlikely to interest my opponent. The move played is an optimistic decision. Better was 15 0-0-0, when his king

would enjoy some kind of shelter. An all-out attack by White is unlikely to be successful in this position.

15	...	♖c8
16	♘e4	♘xe3
17	fxe3	c5
18	♖f1	

At this stage 18 dxc5 ♗xc5 19 ♕xd8 ♖fxd8 would be an attempt to bail out, although White's shattered pawns and misplaced rook on g3 mean that Black has a clear advantage.

18	...	cxd4
19	exd4	♘d5

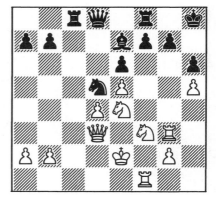

It is now clear that White's king is in the greater danger. White should have bailed out earlier, possibly by exchanging queens. However this kind of strategy is not often used by a G.M. playing in a weekend tournament.

| 20 | ♘fd2 | ♘b4 |

21	♕e3	♘c2
22	♕f4	♘xd4+
23	♔d1	♖c1+

It is significant that it took me a long time to notice this move and shows just how nervous I must have been.

24	♔xc1	♘e2+
25	♔b1	♘xf4
26	♖xf4	♗g5

The technical problems are not too great, as if White continues 27 ♘xg5 ♕xd2 28 ♘xf7+ ♖xf7 29 ♖xf7 ♕d1 is mate. Hence Plaskett has to give up an additional exchange and the game ends swiftly.

27	♖xg5	hxg5
28	♖f3	♕d4
29	♖g3	♕g1+
30	♔c2	♖c8+
31	♔b3	♕b6+
32	♔a3	♖c2

White resigns

Michael followed this success with a win against Chris Beaumont (BFC 210) and he was able to enjoy the luxury of a quick draw in the final round to emerge as an outright winner. This was probably his best success so far, with a tournament grading of 240.

During the Christmas holidays, Michael travelled to New York for his first experience of matchplay. The National Westminster Bank and the Collins Kids sponsored a six game match against Ilya Gurevich, the leading Under 14 in the United States and the holder of the World Under 14 title, although few Europeans had played in that event. The match was played at the home of the legendary John Collins, who had coached Bobby Fischer in his early days and whose home was a true chess museum, according to Mike O'Hara, who accompanied Michael for the match. The player with the white pieces won every game, as Michael's Caro Kann Defence took a pounding.

Michael returned from America to regain the Cornwall Championship, having been unable to compete in the previous season. He continued to support the local chess scene and on March 15th, 1986, Cornwall had their big day. As I have explained, team wins were rare owing to the limited playing strength and the reluctance to travel long distances for just one game. When Cornwall did win, it was against Dorset or Wiltshire and not against the "big boys" like Somerset, Gloucestershire, Hampshire and Devon. However on the given date, Cornwall beat Devon for the first time ever and did so by virtue of a clear win of 10½ to 5½ and even then Cornwall defaulted on one board. Michael did his little bit by defeating George Wheeler on top board.

The Easter holidays were even busier than usual with four big tournaments in less than four weeks. The first of these was at Exeter for the East Devon Congress. Michael won the event outright with four and a half points from his five games. Unfortunately no titled players participated but as usual there was a strong contingent of Bristol players and Michael's win against Alan Ashby in Round Four was the decisive result.

From Exeter, it was on to Weston-super-Mare for his fourth outing in the West of England Championship. We hoped that third and second in the last two years was an indication of how things were going, but we had not anticipated his complete domination of the event. Michael had virtually won the event with two rounds to spare and his five wins came in 26, 19, 23, 36 and 35 moves respectively to lead by a point and a half.

Game 33   28.3.86
Adams-M.Cowling (BCF 194)
West of England Championship
Round Three
Sicilian Defence

1	e4	c5
2	♘f3	d6
3	d4	cxd4
4	♘xd4	♘f6
5	♘c3	a6
6	♗g5	e6
7	f4	♗e7
8	♕f3	♕c7
9	0-0-0	♘bd7
10	g4	b5
11	♗xf6	♘xf6
12	g5	♘d7
13	f5	♗xg5+
14	♔b1	♘e5
15	♕h5	

(see diagram)

15	...	b4

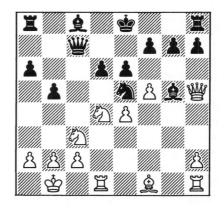

The first departure from theory brings the decisive blunder. 15 ... ♗f6 is the correct move, when 16 ♘xe6 ♗xe6 17 fxe6 g6 18 exf7+ ♔xf7 19 ♕e2 is roughly equal.

16	♕xg5	bxc3
17	♕xg7	♖f8
18	♗b5+	

After 18 ... axb5 19 ♘xb5, the

following 20 ♘xd6+ will be fatal.

| 18 | ... | ♗d7 |
| 19 | fxe6 | axb5 |

No better is 19 ... ♗xb5 20 e7, followed by 21 ♘f5, with another massacre on the d6 square.

| 20 | exd7+ | ♔xd7 |
| 21 | ♘xb5 | ♖xa2 |

Desperation. Black was hopelessly lost in any case.

| 22 | ♘xc7 | ♖xb2+ |
| 23 | ♔a1 | Resigns |

For good measure he defeated Gary Lane in Round Six to make it absolutely certain and to displace him as the youngest ever winner of the event and then went on to a final record breaking score of six and a half out of seven.

The next event was the prestigious Oakham Junior International event. There was a very strong field and Michael could have done with a good start, but unfortunately the reverse happened and he lost his first two games. In the first, he declined a draw offer from Pavel Blatny (FIDE 2415) and went on to lose. He was then paired with Viswanathan Anand (FIDE 2405) and was decisively beaten. Despite averaging fifty per cent over the final seven games, he could never get back into the top half of the tournament and it was a rather disappointing result.

On the following day, he travelled to London for the Lloyds Bank BCF Junior Squad event. As he had won the Under 18 Championship in the previous season, Michael entered the Under 21 section and won it, which was a wonderful result, when it is remembered that he could have been playing in the Under 14 group.

Thus passed the Easter holidays. At half-term, it was off to Gloucester for the Cotswold Open. Another first place resulted, although it was shared with Gary Anthony, with four wins and two draws each. From Gloucester, we drove on to Uppingham, where Michael joined the England Junior Squad, who were taking on World Champion Gary Kasparov in a simultaneous.

Game 34 27.5.86	1	c4	e5
G.Kasparov-Adams	2	♘c3	♘f6
Simultaneous against	3	♘f3	♘c6
English Junior Squad	4	e3	♗b4
English Opening	5	♕c2	0-0

Better here is 5 ... ♗xc3 6 ♕xc3 ♕e7, as I played against Daniel King in the British Championship 1990.

6	♘d5	♖e8
7	♕f5	d6
8	♘xf6+	♕xf6

8 ... gxf6 would have been more ambitious, but also more risky. White has been shown to have an advantage after 9 ♕h5 d5 10 ♗d3 e4 11 cxd5 exd3 12 dxc6, when Black's shattered pawns are a problem. My move gave Black a solid but slightly inferior position.

9	♕xf6	gxf6
10	a3	♗c5
11	b4	♗b6
12	d3	a5
13	b5	♘e7

Also possible was 13 ... ♘b8, with the idea of developing the knight to c5 via d7.

| 14 | ♗e2 | f5 |

Better was 14 ... d5 or 14 ... a4, attempting to fix White's queenside pawns.

| 15 | ♗b2 | ♘g6 |
| 16 | h4! | |

Showing the error of my plan. The knight cannot find a secure post on g6, which would have enabled the pawn-break ... f4.

| 16 | ... | ♘f8 |

17	h5	a4
18	♔f1	♘e6
19	g3	♔f8

More consistent would have been 19 ... ♘c5, aiming to land on the weak b3 square.

20	d4	f6
21	♖d1	h6
22	c5	♗a5
23	♘h4	♘g7

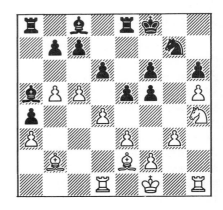

| 24 | b6 | |

This breakthrough is a classic example of undermining a pawn chain. Kasparov has exploited the awkward position of my bishop and the weakness of the doubled f-pawns.

24	...	♗e6
25	bxc7	♗xc7
26	cxd6	♗xd6
27	dxe5	♗xe5
28	♘g6+	♔g8
29	♘xe5	fxe5

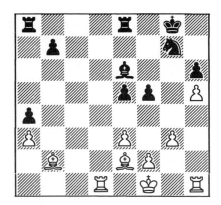

The World Champion has clarified his advantage. His raking
bishop on b2 and superior pawn
structure are very strong. I fought
well, after being strategically outplayed in the opening, but my
opponent's advantage is so secure,
that it is unlikely to be destroyed
by anything other than a bad
mistake, which Kasparov is not
renowned for.

30	♖h4	e4
31	g4	♖e7
32	gxf5	♗xf5
33	♖f4	♖f8
34	♔e1	♔h7
35	♗c4	

A bad slip, not noticing that the
bishop was tied to the defence of
the h-pawn. However, it is not
enough to change the course of
the game and merely gave me
another weak pawn to defend. 35
♖d5 is a stronger continuation.

35	...	♘xh5
36	♖h4	♗g6
37	♖d6	♘g7
38	♖b6	h5
39	♖h1	♘f5
40	♗e2	

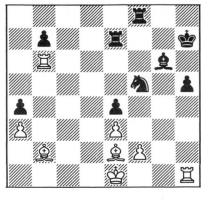

| 40 | ... | h4 |

Overambitious. I cannot sustain
the pawn here and should have
played 40... ♘g7, although White
is in control anyhow.

41	♗g4	♖c7
42	♖b4	♖ff7
43	♗d1	

43 ♗xf5 is possible, regaining
the h-pawn. However he prefers
to pick off the other pawns first.

43	...	♔h6
44	♖xe4	b5
45	♖b4	♖c4
46	♖xb5	♖e7
47	♗e2	♖c2
48	♗d3	**Resigns**

Gary Kasparov went on to win by 14 points to 6, with Philip Rossiter, David Watts and Philip Morris our only winners.

A second Glorney Cup appearance was made in Ireland. He was moved up to Board Two below Neil Carr. Again he won four and drew one of his games to help England retain the trophy, although a 5½ to ½ victory against the Netherlands was necessary before success was clinched.

Michael left Dublin early on Saturday morning, flew to Bristol and caught a train back to Cornwall to arrive in mid-afternoon. Clothes were thrown into the washing machine, dried, ironed and re-packed. Then on Sunday morning, we were all driving up to Southampton for the British Championships. Although Michael's rating had dropped to 2260, his success in the West of England Championship had earned him qualification. On Monday, play commenced.

Looking back, I realise that it was not the best way to prepare for the most important tournament of the season, but at the time, we never gave it any thought. We were guided by the principle that you grabbed as much chess as you could in the school holidays. It never occurred to us to decline the Glorney invitation to concentrate on proper preparation. It was just as well that Michael possessed great reserves of stamina.

Less was expected of Michael this year as his rating had slumped to 2260 and he enjoyed the luxury of going into every game as the underdog. This took all the pressure off Michael and he thoroughly enjoyed himself. He made a great start, defeating Jonathan Levitt (FIDE 2455) with Black in the first round and followed that up by beating Karl Bowden (FIDE 2340).

I had not been at the chess for the first two days, having been touring the area with Margaret and Janet, but I decided to go along on the Wednesday as it was the first time that Michael had ever appeared on the top four boards of the Championship. That meant two things – firstly that the moves of his game would appear on a large display board so that I would be able to follow the game without going near the board and secondly that the game was likely to be featured in the commentary room. As I had not been able to understand what was going on in Michael's games for some time, I hoped that Graham Lee and Malcolm Pein would be able to make it clear what was happening in his game against David Norwood (FIDE 2415). Unfortunately the commentators were not very impressed with the opening play of the two juniors and some amusing comments were made at their expense. A suggestion was made that two life-like dummies had been substituted for the real players, who had gone off to enjoy themselves elsewhere. It was good entertainment and I did not mind at all, but poor Graham was quite embarrassed when he found out that I was in the audience.

Actually the game livened up later, although it was agreed drawn in the adjournment session. Another hard earned draw against Tony Kosten (FIDE 2455) followed and then Michael defeated Stuart Conquest (FIDE 2415). An exciting draw with Jim Plaskett (FIDE 2450) followed in which both players missed a winning chance. Thus Michael had gone through the first week undefeated, including two wins and two draws against International Masters and a draw against a Grandmaster.

Most British Championship competitors enjoy a well deserved rest on Sunday, especially if they are up with the leaders. However when Michael was presented with a choice between a day trip to the Isle of Wight with his family and a seven round quickplay, he opted for the latter without a moment's hesitation. It proved to be a sound choice as he remained dry while winning seven straight games at the Guildhall while the rest of us experienced the English summer at its worst and were deluged by incessant rain.

Such chess overtime did not appear to do him much harm as he defeated another International Master, Willie Watson, to better his Edinburgh score and joined Grandmasters Speelman, Chandler and Mestel in the lead.

Game 35   4.8.86
W.Watson (FIDE 2495)-Adams
British Championship
Round Seven
French Defence

1	e4	e6
2	d4	d5
3	♘c3	♝b4
4	♗d3	

Not as critical as the main line 4 e5. White was probably happy to take the game into uncharted territory, rather than to into a critical theoretical variation. I was also happy with this choice.

4	...	dxe4
5	♗xe4	♘f6
6	♗d3	

6 ♗f3 c5 7 ♘ge2 has also been played but these positions are not particularly dangerous for Black.

6	...	c5
7	a3	♝a5

After 7 ... ♝xc3+ 8 bxc3, the two bishops would give White

some attacking chances, but after the game move, White must allow the shattering of his pawn structure, ensuring a good game for Black.

8	dxc5	♝xc3+
9	bxc3	♞bd7
10	♝e3	♛c7
11	♞f3	0-0
12	0-0	e5
13	♞d2	♞xc5
14	♝g5	

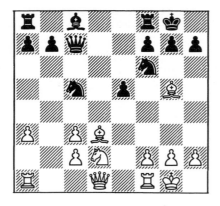

14	...	e4

Perhaps I could have played more ambitiously here with 14 ... ♞d5, but it suited me to take the game into a fairly drawish position, as I was still somewhat in awe of opponents like Willie Watson.

15	♝xf6	exd3
16	♝d4	dxc2
17	♛xc2	♞e6
18	♝e3	b6
19	f4	

Undoubtedly my opponent wanted to push for more than a draw to sustain his British Championship bid, but this move was risky, as it allows my queen's bishop an extremely powerful diagonal.

19	...	♝a6
20	♜fe1	♜ad8!

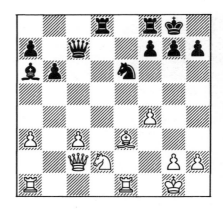

I am now penetrating on d3 and White has the problem of defending his f4 pawn. Probably he should have played 20 ♜f2.

21	♛a4	♞c5
22	♛c2	♞d3
23	♜f1	♜fe8
24	♜f3	♝b7
25	♜h3	g6
26	♜f1	

(see diagram)

26	...	♜xe3!

The decisive tactic, which left me with two very strong minor pieces for an ineffective rook.

Michael one move ahead of his dad.

Giving his first simultaneous display at Falmouth Chess Club as a ten year old. He won 21 and lost two of his games.

Only eleven and Michael defeats three computers at a special challenge in Plymouth.

Analysing with Boris Spassky after their Quickplay "curtain raiser" to Lloyds Bank Masters 1984.

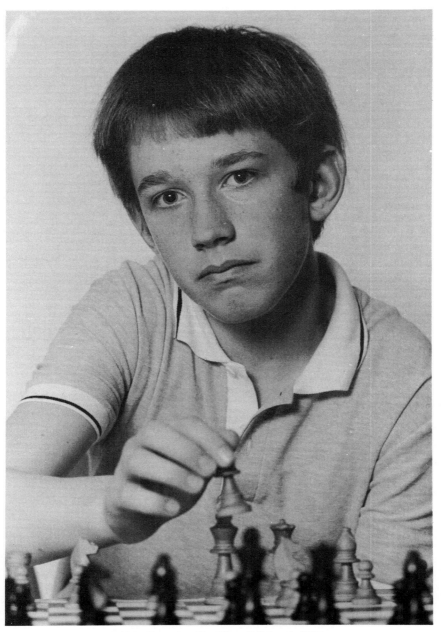

British Championship début, Edinburgh 1985.

A study in concentration.

At Ostende, 1989.

Michael Adams — Grandmaster!

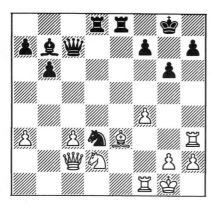

28	♘c4	b5
29	♔h1	bxc4
30	♕e2	♝c6
31	f5	♖b8
32	♖g3	♖e8
33	♕d2	♕e5
34	fxg6	hxg6
35	♕h6	♕f5!

A neat back rank trick effectively finishes the game. If 36 ♔g1 ♕xf1+ 37 ♔xf1 ♖e1 mate.

36	♖a1	♘e1
37	♔g1	♖e2
38	♖d1	♕f2+

White resigns

27 ♖xe3   ♕c5

Suddenly there was rash talk of Michael winning the event, which was something that neither Michael nor myself remotely considered, especially when we looked at who the co-leaders were. Jonathan Mestel justified our outlook by defeating Michael in the next round.

Nevertheless draws with Devaki Prasad (FIDE 2410) and Neil McDonald (FIDE 2495) clinched an IM norm with a round to spare. It was quite amazing as we did not really know what an IM norm was when the tournament began. Apparently Michael became only the sixth fourteen year old to achieve such a feat, the others being Fischer, Mecking, Short, Anand and Saeed. What was particularly pleasing was that it had been achieved in a fierce, competitive atmosphere.

For good measure, he drew his last game with another International Master, Julian Hodgson (FIDE 2500), which meant that he shared sixth place and the British Under 21 title.

Then it was home to Cornwall for a week of surf, sea, sand and sun before another trip to London for Lloyds Bank events as well as a visit to the Park Lane Hotel, where Kasparov and Karpov were playing the first half of their world title clash. As one of the sideshows, Michael gave a simultaneous display and made a lot of people happy, as he conceded a string of defeats.

However he was not in such a generous mood when he walked away with the Under 21 BCF Squad Quickplay, scoring nine wins and a draw to win the event by one and a half points, ahead of quite a strong field. Again, it has to be emphasised that he was by far the youngest player in the event and also that his opponents were strong players.

He began the Masters event well by defeating Devaki Prasad, who had just won the Commonwealth title, in the first round. A draw against Stuart Conquest and wins against Pia Cramling and Y.Kosashvili followed to put Michael within reach of a second IM norm, which was eventually achieved when he defeated Neil McDonald in Round Eight after a 94 move marathon. Thus he repeated his British Championship performance in having a round to spare.

By this time, we had found out about IM norms and titles and realised that one more norm would give him the title, but the regulations stated that it had to be achieved in an all-play-all event. As fortune would have it, such an event, sponsored by the National Westminster Bank was about to take place. Unfortunately it was by invitation only and despite my polite enquiry, no invitation was given to Michael as his current rating of 2260 was considered too low.

It was very disappointing, especially as Michael had seemed to hit a period of very fine results and might well have completed the title requirements. Still, we had never contemplated being in such a position at the beginning of the school holidays and another year lay ahead. There was no doubt what the next target was.

9 Runner-Up in World Under 16

At the beginning of the new season, Michael was approaching his fifteenth birthday and his BCF grade had risen to 219, which put him among the top fifty players in Britain. The previous season's results had shown that he was capable of holding his own against all but the very top English players. This had all been achieved with a very amateurish approach, apart from the limited amount of coaching by Shaun Taulbut, which had ceased over four years earlier. There should have been a more professional approach from this point and I feel guilty that there was not, but it is easier to make the point than see what we could have done about it. Besides Michael was quite happy, so we carried on quite unconcerned as Michael entered the fourth year at Truro School and started his GCSE courses.

He made a disappointing start to the season, opting for the weekend British Isles Open at Swansea, rather than the slower pace of the Paignton event and proceeded to lose to a couple of players with grades in the region of 175, namely R.Saunders and M.Binks, in Rounds One and Three.

His next event was the Hexagon Open at the Plymouth Guildhall, which he won outright for a second successive year. Most of the leading West Country players were among the twenty four competitors in the Open, but there were few visitors from further afield. Michael did drop a half point to Chris Butt in Round One, but then worked through the field, defeating Alan Ashby and Philip Rossiter in the last two rounds.

Two draws conceded to K.Hyde (BCF 179) and Gerald Moore (BCF 193) gave him too much to pull back at the Torbay Open and left him in second place, half a point behind the winner, Gary Lane. It was slightly puzzling and worrying that too high a proportion of Michael's lost points came from games where he had the white pieces and this was so in both drawn games here. His only win with the white pieces came in the final round.

Game 36   23.11.86
Adams-N.Crickmore (BCF 192)
Torbay Open
Round Five
French Defence

1	e4	e6
2	d4	d5
3	♘d2	♘f6
4	e5	♘fd7
5	c3	c5
6	f4	♘c6
7	♘df3	cxd4
8	cxd4	♕b6
9	g3	♗b4+
10	♔f2	g5
11	fxg5	

Also possible in this position is
11 ♗e3.

11	...	♘dxe5
12	♔g2	

Better in this sharp variation of
the French Defence is 12 ♘xe5
♘xe5 13 ♗e3, when 13 ... ♘c6 14
♘f3 ♗d7 15 ♖c1 is better for
White. The critical move is 13 ...
♘c4.

12	...	♘g6

More accurate is 12 ... ♘xf3 13
♘xf3 ♗f8!, with chances for both
sides. My opponent did play this
line against me at Exeter four
months later.

13	h4	♗d7
14	h5	♘ge7
15	♘e2	♗d6

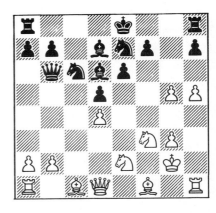

16   ♕b3!

Although I enjoy a superior
pawn structure, I have to be careful
that early pawn advances do not
expose my king too much. The
exchange of queens gives me a
promising ending.

16	...	♕xb3

More dynamic would have been
16 ... ♕c7 17 ♗f4 with a difficult
position for both sides.

17	axb3	a6
18	♗d2	♖c8
19	♖c1	♘b4
20	♖xc8+	♗xc8
21	♘f4	♗d7
22	♘d3	♘ec6
23	♘xb4	♘xb4

Although my opponent has
maintained an outpost on b4, in
reality it is not very important.

24	♗e2	♔e7

25	♖c1	♘c6

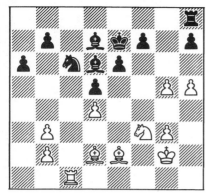

Now that I have mobilised my pieces, Black's weaknesses are revealed, especially the pawn on h7, which requires the protection of the rook, which would be more profitably occupied on other matters.

26	♗d3	♗b8

A clever move, aiming to bring pressure against the d4 pawn and threatening 27 ... ♗a7 28 ♗e3 e5, thus forcing my next move. It is a long gradual process to relieve myself from defending this pawn, but his rook is paralysed.

27	♔f2	♗a7
28	♗e3	♗b6
29	♗b1	♘a5
30	♖c3	♘c6
31	♖d3	♗e8

32	♖d1	♗d7

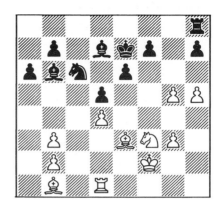

33 h6

At last, I am ready to execute the winning plan. First, I fix the pawn on h7, before continuing with ♗f4, ♔e3, ♘e5. Against this plan, Black has no good reply.

33	...	♗e8
34	♗f4	♗d7
35	♔e3	♗e8
36	♘e5	♘xd4

Desperation, as if 36 ... ♘b4 37 ♘g4, with the idea of moving to ♘f6, wins the h-pawn.

37	♖xd4	f5
38	gxf6+	♔xf6
39	♘f3	♗g6

and Black resigned

He overlooked 40 ♗e5+, but the game was lost in any event.

Michael was rarely able to accept his invitation to participate in the

ARC Young Masters event, but on this occasion the Friday night round coincided with our half-term week so we set off for Uppingham. Michael finished a respectable fifth equal, behind Nigel Davies, Murray Chandler, David Norwood and Chris Baker, despite dropping one and a half points with his first two Whites against Christine Flear and T.Enqvist (Sweden).

Game 37   28.2.87
R.Willmoth (BCF 205)-Adams
A.R.C. Young Masters
Round Four
French Defence

1	e4	e6
2	d4	d5
3	e5	c5
4	c3	♘c6
5	♘f3	♗d7
6	a3	

The idea of this move is to play b4 and take the pressure off White's centre by removing the tension on d4. It is not good to prevent this with 6 ... a5 as after 7 ♗d3 the two pawn moves favour White.

6	...	c4
7	g3	f6

This move is not considered the best, but it creates more interesting positions and gives both players more winning chances than the approved 7 ... ♕b6.

8 exf6

It is not clear that this exchange is favourable for White as it allows me to develop my pieces quickly. The simple 8 ♗g2 is better.

8	...	♘xf6
9	♗g2	♗d6
10	0-0	0-0
11	♖e1	

White needs to be more careful as his f2 square is weakened by this move. Better was 11 ♘bd2, with the idea of 12 b3.

11	...	♕b6
12	♕e2	♖ae8
13	♘e5	

With ... e5 a serious worry, White does not have many good alternatives, but this is clearly incorrect. 13 ♗e3 was better.

13	...	♗xe5
14	dxe5	

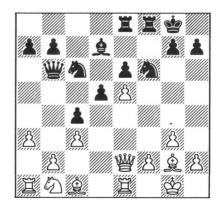

14	...	♘g4!

This refutes White's previous play. Of course, if 15 ♕xg4? ♕xf2+.

15	♗f4	♘gxe5
16	b4	♘d3
17	♗e3	d4!

After this move, I hold an overwhelming material advantage. My opponent fights hard, but the result is never in doubt.

18	cxd4	♘xe1
19	♕xe1	♘xd4
20	♘c3	e5
21	♕d1	♗c6
22	♘e4	♕d8
23	♖b1	b5

24	♕h5	♕a8!

White has no real threats on the kingside, so I can put pressure on the long diagonal, h1-a8.

25	♕g4	♘e2+
26	♔h1	♘c3
27	♗h6	♖e7

The final trick was 27 ... ♖f7 28 ♘f6+.

28	♖e1	♘xe4
29	♗xe4	♗xe4+
30	♖xe4	♖f4
31	gxf4	♕xe4+
32	f3	♕e1+
33	♔g2	exf4
34	♕c8+	♖e8
	White resigns	

East Devon was a tournament much nearer home and could be reached for the Friday night round after a day at school. Having won the event for the first time in the previous season, he repeated the process for three more years, although on this occasion a maximum score could only earn first equal in a very strong field, including one GM, one WGM and two IMs. International Master Daniel King shared first place with Michael. Perhaps it was just as well that there was not a sixth round as Michael had recently been selected to play in the World Under 16 event and had asked for Daniel to be his second.

It was the first time that we had been asked to make such a choice, although we had asked Mike O'Hara to accompany Michael to New York. We had been extremely happy with that arrangement, but unfortunately Mike was not a strong enough player to accompany Michael to Innsbruck for the World Under 16, although in many other ways he would have been a good choice. Ideally there should be someone concentrating on Junior Chess, who would have followed Michael's progress so far and be familiar with his ways on and off the chess board, who would automatically have taken on such a role. Instead Michael went off with a comparative stranger, who did an excellent job, but could not build on the relationship that he had established as he had his own career to follow.

Anyway to return to East Devon, Michael's result was a fine 247 performance, with the final three rounds producing wins against Neil Crickmore, Chris Ward and Philip Rossiter. Michael was certainly getting his own back for all the early defeats that he suffered at Philip's hands.

Michael also successfully defended his Lloyds Bank BCF Junior Squad Under 21 title, which was particularly pleasing, with three established International Masters, Stuart Conquest, Neil McDonald and James Howell, in the field. It remained a constant thorn in the flesh that Michael could not have the chance to gain his final norm when we considered that he was good enough to deserve the title. The decisive game was played in Round Five, although before then, Michael had beaten M.Fraser (BCF 198), Philip Morris (BCF 204) and A.Tucker (BCF 182), as well as drawing with Stuart Conquest (BCF 232).

Game 38   5.4.87
N.McDonald (BCF 225)-**Adams**
BCF Lloyds Bank Squad Under 21
Round Five
French Defence

1	e4	e6
2	d4	d5
3	♘c3	♗b4
4	e5	♘e7
5	♘f3	c5
6	a3	♗xc3+
7	bxc3	♕a5
8	♗d2	♘bc6
9	c4	♕c7
10	cxd5	♘xd5
11	c3	♗d7
12	♗e2	0-0-0
13	0-0	f6

| 14 | c4 | ♘de7 |
| 15 | exf6 | gxf6 |

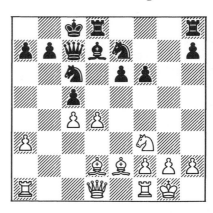

This position is quite well known and Black has good chances after the more normal 16 dxc5 e5. The move played has been suggested but it does not appear that White gains sufficient compensation for the sacrificed pawn.

16	d5	exd5
17	cxd5	♞xd5
18	♛b3	

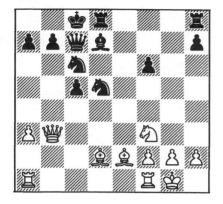

| **18** | **...** | **♖hg8!** |

A strong continuation, not yet defending the knight on d5, as 19 ♛xd5 would be met by 19 ... ♝h3. After 18 ... ♝e6 19 ♝c4, White would have had more compensation.

19 ♖fc1

19 ♝c4 was also possible here, but Black has a good reply in 19 ...

♞ce7 preparing ♝c6. Again 20 ♝xd5 ♞xd5 21 ♛xd5 ♝h3 is no good for White.

19	...	♝h3
20	♞h4	♝g4
21	♝xg4+	♖xg4
22	♞f5	♛d7
23	♖ab1	♞b6

It now becomes clear that White must part with a piece for very poor compensation.

24	♖xc5	♛xd2
25	♞e7+	♚c7
26	h3	♖g5
27	♖xg5	♛xg5
28	♞xc6	bxc6
29	♛c2	♛g6

The position has clarified and the lack of compensation is confirmed. I made no mistakes in finishing the job.

30	♛b3	♛d3
31	♛b2	♛d4
32	♛c2	♖d7
33	♛f5	♛e5
34	♛f3	f5
35	♖c1	♛e4
36	♛c3	♚b7
37	♖e1	♛d4
38	♛b3	f4

White resigns

Another successful title defence was made at the West of England Championship, although this was achieved in rather unorthodox fashion as he lost his first round game with the white pieces against R.Heasman (BCF 188). Fortunately it was a seven round event and this gave Michael sufficient time to overhaul those in front of him, overtaking the leader in the final round by defeating him.

Michael had to take time off school for the World Under 16 event, but as I explained earlier that was a rare occurrence. However we felt that this was too important a chance to miss. Michael made a great effort to win the event. Indeed his score of nine points out of eleven would have won the event in most years, but on this occasion it meant the runner-up spot and the silver medal.

All of Michael's games ended decisively, with nine wins and two defeats. Ironically it was Michael's determination to go for wins that cost him the title. In their Round Four game, Michael avoided an obvious drawing opportunity against Hannes Stefansson (Iceland), the eventual champion, and made what turned out to be an inferior move and lost. Nevertheless with five straight wins, Michael regained the lead, only to lose to Daniel Moldovan (Romania), despite having a clear advantage at one stage.

All six games with Black were won and his defeats were again with White – a far cry from his White-dominated match with Ilya Gurevich, but at least White's superiority continued in their games.

Game 39 16.5.87	9	♗h3	cxd4
Adams-I.Gurevich (FIDE 2410)	10	cxd4	f6
World Under 16	11	♔f1	fxe5
Round Six	12	fxe5	0-0
French Defence	13	♔g2	

1   e4   e6

A different defence to those played in our match of White domination.

2	d4	d5
3	♘d2	♘f6
4	e5	♘fd7
5	c3	c5
6	f4	♘c6
7	♘df3	♕b6
8	g3	♗e7

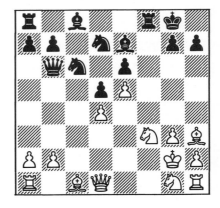

In this position, the piece sacrifice 13 ... ♘dxe5 14 fxe5 ♘xe5 is probably the best continuation. The move played leaves Black very cramped for no real compensation.

| 13 | ... | ♔h8 |
| 14 | ♗g4! | |

Now White's king has the escape square on h3, sacrifices on e5 are no longer possible. When I have unravelled my pieces, I should stand clearly better, due to the large space advantage.

| 14 | ... | ♘d8 |

It was more important to improve the positioning of the other knight. Better here would have been 14 ... ♘db8.

15	h4	♘f7
16	♘e2	♘h6
17	♗h3	

Also possible, and probably better, was 17 ♗xh6 gxh6 18 ♕d2.

| 17 | ... | ♘f5 |
| 18 | ♕c2 | ♕c6 |

Black has to hurry the exchange of the queens as ♗xf5, with the idea of ♗g5 or ♘g5, is an attractive proposition. Black should have taken time earlier to improve the position of his passively placed knight on d7.

| 19 | ♕d3 | ♕c4 |
| 20 | ♕xc4 | dxc4 |

| 21 | ♘f4 | ♘b6 |

While it may appear that Black has solved his problems by exchanging the queens, White is actually able to inaugurate a forced sequence of moves, which obtain a favourable ending.

22	♗xf5	♖xf5
23	g4	♖f8
24	♘g5	♗xg5
25	hxg5	♔g8

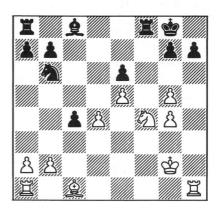

The ending is pleasant for me, owing to the half open h-file and my greater space. The opposite coloured bishops do not greatly increase Black's chances of drawing with so many pieces on the board.

| 26 | ♗d2 | ♗d7 |
| 27 | ♔g3 | g6 |

Black was threatened by ♗b4, when ♖f7 would be impossible due to g6. Better, however, was 27 ... ♘d5.

| 28 | ♖af1 | ♖f7 |
| 29 | ♗a5 | ♘d5 |

Black does not want to reach an ending in which his traditionally bad bishop on d7 is dominated by White's knight, although objectively this was a better chance than the game continuation. Gurevich chose to seek refuge in the rook and opposite coloured bishops ending. Perhaps Black should have played 28 ... ♖e7.

| 30 | ♘xd5 | ♖xf1 |

Of course 30 ... exd5 31 ♖xf7 ♔xf7 32 ♖xh7+ ♔e6 33 ♗b4 ♖e8 34 ♖g7 holds no hope for Black. Hence he is forced to allow the extremely powerful passed pawn on f6.

31	♘f6+	♖xf6
32	gxf6	♗c6
33	♖h2	♖f8

34	♔f4	♖f7
35	♗b4	♖d7
36	♗d6	b5
37	♔g5	a5
38	a3	♗f3

Although this move loses to a forced tactical sequence, better defensive attempts only delay the inevitable.

39	♖f2	♗c6
40	♗e7	♔f7
41	♖h2	♔g8
42	f7+	♔xf7
43	♖xh7+	♔g8
44	♔h6	♖b7
45	♖g7+	♔h8
46	♖f7	♖b8
47	♖h7+	♔g8
48	♖g7+	**Resigns**

At the end, my opponent was powerless to stop me executing a straightforward plan to victory.

When the school summer term was completed, he travelled to Charlton and tried to repeat his West of England tactics by losing the first round to Andrew Mack (BCF 180) and trying to catch up. It was not quite successful on this occasion as it was only a six round event and five straight wins only moved him as far as second place, despite good wins against Chris Ward (BCF 211) and Nigel Davies (BCF 234) in the final two rounds.

Michael made his final Glorney Cup appearance at Swansea, appearing on Board One. Although his age would have permitted him three more appearances, it was clear that he was not gaining great experience from the event. Still he did enjoy helping England to another triumph by contributing three wins and a draw from his four games to make his complete Glorney record eleven wins, three draws and no defeats.

By this time, Michael's rating had returned to 2360 and we realised that the British Championship would be a difficult assignment. It was unlikely that he would repeat the Southampton result, while he would outrate most of his opponents and be expected to beat them, thus increasing the pressure on Michael.

However he started even better than at Southampton, accumulating four and a half points from his first five games. Colin McNab (FIDE 2435), Jim Plaskett (FIDE 2475) and Julian Hodgson (FIDE 2510) were three of his victims. This earned him a first clash with Nigel Short.

Game 40   8.8.87
Adams-N.Short (FIDE 2620)
British Championship
Round Six
Ruy Lopez

1	e4	e5
2	♘f3	♘c6
3	♗b5	a6
4	♗a4	♘f6
5	0-0	♗e7
6	♖e1	b5
7	♗b3	d6
8	c3	0-0
9	h3	♘d7
10	d4	♗f6
11	a4	♗b7
12	♘a3	

Not an accurate continuation. It never really threatened to help to capture on b5 due to the pin down the a-file. Theory suggests 12 d5.

12	...	exd4
13	cxd4	♖e8
14	♕d2	

A strange looking move, but I

had to cope with the threat of ... ♘b4.

14	...	♖e7
15	♗c2	♕e8
16	b3	

If now 16 ♖b1 b4 17 ♘c4 d5, Black has no problems.

16	...	bxa4
17	bxa4	a5!

This secures the b4 square for Black's knight and this turns out to be very important.

18 ♗b1

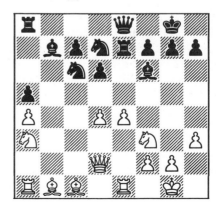

Better was 18 ♘b5. I overlooked my opponent's reply.

| 18 | ... | ♘c5 |
| 19 | e5 | |

The complications created by this move are favourable for Black, but it seemed preferable to me to enduring the existing situation.

19	...	dxe5
20	♕c2	e4
21	♗g5	♗xg5
22	♘xg5	♘d3
23	♖xe4	♖xe4
24	♕xd3	

24 ♘xe4 lost immediately to the strong reply 24 ... ♘cb4. Hence White is forced to part with material.

24	...	♖e1+
25	♔h2	g6
26	♗a2	

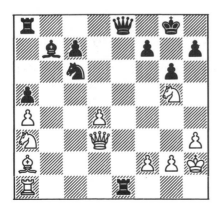

Although Black is the exchange

up for nothing, it is not hopeless for me as there is a mutual time shortage and my pieces are quite active, so I can try some traps. However opponents of this calibre do not find it too much trouble avoiding them.

26	...	♖e7
27	♖e1	♘d8
28	♖b1	♕c6
29	d5	♕d6+
30	♔g1	

Better was 30 g3, although the position is lost in any case.

30	...	♕f4
31	h4	♕xh4
32	♕d2	♗a6
33	♘b5	♗xb5
34	♖xb5	♕xa4
35	♖b3	

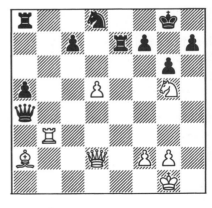

| 35 | ... | ♖a6 |
| 36 | ♖b8 | |

36 ♘xh7 ♔xh7 37 ♖h3+ ♔g8

38 ♕h6 ♕d4 is not dangerous for
Black, either.

36	...	♖d6
37	♖c8	♕b4
38	♕xb4	axb4

39	f3	♔g7
40	♘e4	b3
41	♗xb3	♖b6
42	♗a4	♘b7
43	♗c6	♘d6

White resigns

Again Michael opted to play the Sunday Quickplay rather than face the rigours of a day out with the family or any alternative relaxation. He did win the event, but the critics who said that he should have kept away from the chess on the middle Sunday undoubtedly seemed to have a point, especially when Michael lost to Craig Pritchett (FIDE 2365) on the following day. Personally I do not think that it made any difference, but, as always, the final decision was left to Michael.

He recovered to beat Andrew Martin (FIDE 2375), but then lost to Igor Ivanov (FIDE 2500). However a good finish with a draw against James Howell (FIDE 2375) and a final round win against Dene Hergott (FIDE 2305) ensured that he equalled his Southampton score and again finished sixth equal, although Stuart Conquest won the Under 21 title outright. For what it was worth, it earned him another IM norm, which he could not use, as it was only an all-play-all norm that would enable him to complete his title requirements.

Michael did not travel back to Cornwall with the rest of the family, but headed for London to try to qualify for the final rounds of the British Speed Championships. He was very disappointed to finish just half a point behind the qualifiers, mainly because of his defeat by Viswanathan Anand (India).

The same player also defeated Michael at the Lloyds Bank Masters. However a tournament result of seven points out of ten was his best Masters result so far and his final round win against the Israeli, I.Manor, ensured that he finished seventh equal out of 180 competitors.

It had been another satisfying season. He had played fifteen games against IM and GM players and had emerged with the record of eight wins, three draws and only four defeats (Short, Pritchett, Ivanov and Anand). This was good evidence that he was worthy of the title and it was really frustrating that he had not had the opportunity to complete the requirements.

10 An International Master, At Last!

Michael began the new season by returning to Swansea for the British Isles Open and fared rather better than the previous season. Instead of two defeats in the first three rounds, there were two draws, which were not so harmful and indeed were quite protective in keeping him away from the top players until the last round. He defeated Graham Burgess (BCF 195), Neil Bradbury (BCF 217) and Jim Plaskett (BCF 234) in the final rounds to finish first equal alongside Grandmasters Nunn, Chandler, Rogers (Australia) and Kudrin (USA).

Shortly afterwards, the long awaited all-play-all arrived in the form of the Nat West Young Masters event. It was held three weeks into the new term, but having waited so long, there was no way that we were going to turn it down. We did not know how long Michael might have to wait for another chance.

As it was the first time that he had played in this type of event and as the first round started at 2 p.m. on the Saturday afternoon, I decided to accompany Michael to London and watch a couple of rounds. We caught a train that was scheduled to arrive at 11.30 a.m., but unfortunately it arrived in London over three hours late. Needless to say, when we did arrive at Paddington, there was not a taxi in sight, so we dashed to the tube and I started calculating frantically how long Michael would have to reach the first time control. Michael remained completely unruffled, as if to say that he would cope with whatever was in his control but would accept other things as they happened.

In the event, Keith Arkell had agreed to wait for Michael and the clock had not been started. However there was one disturbing piece of news. The IM norm mark was to be six and a half points out of nine and not six as had previously been planned. The general impression was that it would be quite difficult to reach.

Michael began with two draws with White against Keith Arkell and Gary Lane, but then won four successive games to bring the title within reach – just a point and a half needed from three games. When Andrew

Martin offered a draw in Round Seven after just ten moves, Michael decided to accept it as Andrew was the highest rated of his three remaining opponents and it would have been awful to turn down the draw and go on to lose. I am sure that it was the right decision, but twenty four hours later, he was beginning to regret it as he lost to the Egyptian International Master, Tarek Fatin, after achieving a winning position, throwing it away and then missing opportunities to hold a draw.

Game 41   10.10.87
Adams-T.Fatin (FIDE 2305)
Nat West Young Masters
Round Eight
Sicilian Defence

1	e4	c5
2	♘f3	♘c6
3	♗b5	g6
4	0-0	♗g7
5	♖e1	a6

More common in the closed variation of the Sicilian Defence is 5 ... ♘f6.

6	♗xc6	dxc6
7	♘c3	e5

Whilst the closed centre reached by this move is acceptable for Black in many related positions of the Ruy Lopez, it is not so here as Black takes a long time to manoeuvre his knight to the d4 square. The difference is that in the Ruy Lopez, Black's second c-pawn is on c7, allowing the knight to use the route e7-c6-d4.

8	a4	a5
9	b3	♘e7
10	♗b2	0-0
11	d3	♕c7
12	♔h1	♗d7
13	♕d2	h6
14	♘e2	b6
15	♘fg1	♖ae8
16	f4	

This pawn break is necessary and should be to White's advantage. If Black had played 15 ... f5 16 exf5 gxf5 17 f4 would have been strong.

16	...	exf4
17	♗xg7	♔xg7
18	♘xf4	♘g8
19	♘f3	♗g4
20	♖f1	g5

Not a desirable move for Black, but he is seeking to interrupt the smoothness of my plans. However he is left with weak squares that can be exploited.

21	♘e2	f5
22	exf5	♗xf5
23	♘g3	♗g6

If 23 ... ♗g4, White wins a pawn by 24 ♘xg5.

24	♖ae1	♘f6
25	♖xe8	♖xe8
26	♕c3	♕d6
27	♕a1	

This move was unnecessary. Better was 27 d4 at once.

27	...	♖e6

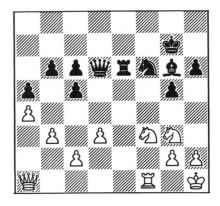

28   d4!

Black seems to have consolidated his position, but this move gives me the edge. It was a brave decision as I only needed one out of two for the norm.

28	...	♔h7
29	dxc5	bxc5
30	♕c3	♘d5
31	♕xa5	♘e3
32	♖e1	g4
33	♘d2	♗xc2

A mistake, which enables me to win two knights for the rook.

34	♕c3	♕d4

35	♖xe3	♖xe3
36	♕xc2+	♖d3
37	♘e2	♕e3
38	♘c4	♕e4
39	♔g1	

It is not going to be easy to convert the point and considerable care must be exercised. This is a sensible move, cutting out back rank tricks.

39	...	♔h8
40	a5	♕d5
41	♕b2+	♔g8

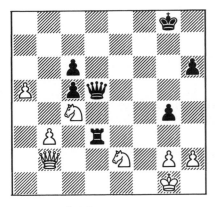

42   ♘f4?

A bad blunder, not anticipating Black's 45th move. After 42 ♕f6, I would be winning.

42	...	♖d1+
43	♔f2	♕e4
44	♕e5	

44 ♔g3 was better, after which White is still winning.

44	...	♖d2+

45	♔g3	♖xg2+
46	♔h4	

Of course 46 ♘xg2 ♕f3+ 47 ♔h4 ♕h3++.

46	...	♖xh2+
47	♔xg4	♖g2+
48	♔h4	♖h2+
49	♔g3	

This is a reckless attempt to go for a win, when I should be satisfied with the draw. 49 ♔g4 should be played.

49	...	♕xe5
50	♘xe5	♖b2
51	♘xc6	♖xb3+
52	♔h4	♖a3
53	♘d5	

This ending should still be drawn, although Black has the advantage. However I was disillusioned with my previous play and continued to make mistakes.

53	...	♔f7
54	♘c7	♖a4+
55	♔h5	c4
56	♘b5	♔g7
57	♘c3	♖a1

58	♔g4	♔h7
59	♘e4	

The fatal mistake, after many wounding ones. If I had passed with my king, it was difficult for my opponent to make progress. Now one of my knights is lost and so is the game.

59	...	c3
60	♘xc3	♖c1
61	a6	♖xc3
62	a7	♖a3
63	♔h4	♖a4+
64	♔h3	♔g7
65	♔g3	♔f6
66	♔h3	♔g5
67	♔g3	♖a3+
68	♔g2	h5
69	♔h2	h4
70	♘e5	♖xa7
71	♘f3+	♔f4
72	♘d4	♔g4
73	♔g2	♖a2+
74	♔g1	♖d2
75	♘b3	♖d5
76	♔h2	h3
77	♘c1	♖d2+
78	♔g1	♔g3
White resigns		

It meant that he now had to win his last game with Black against Francis Rayner. I was glad that I was back in Cornwall and did not have to endure the 69 move struggle that ensued. Chess history is littered with failures to achieve norms by players requiring a win in their last game and several onlookers thought that Michael might have to accept a draw and join them, but Michael never had any doubts and his calmness, especially after the previous day's disaster, impressed everyone and eventually he was triumphant.

By this time Gary Lane had achieved his final norm and won the event, so it was a great West country triumph with Gary and Michael thus becoming the first ever International Masters from Devon and Cornwall respectively. Despite the long wait, Michael also became the youngest current title holder.

His next tournament was the Torbay Open and he won his first four games and then agreed a quick draw with Chris Baker in the final round. Wins against Gerald Moore (BCF 193), George Wheeler (BCF 193) and Chris Beaumont (BCF 211) were achieved in the middle rounds.

Before Christmas, Michael returned to Islington for the first time since his disasters of seven years earlier. It was difficult to believe that it was only seven years as so much had happened in between. On this occasion, Michael finished third equal in the Open, half a point behind Keith Arkell and Murray Chandler, who drew with Michael in Round Four. In the following round, Michael avoided defeat by Mark Hebden for the first time and actually had the better of a draw, and he finished by beating Peter Large.

After Christmas, Michael went down to Hastings for the first time. The slow tempo of one round a day had never appealed to Michael when he was younger, but now there was the combined appeal of adding some rating points and possibly qualifying for the following year's Premier event by winning the Challengers event.

Michael began with four White wins and four Black draws, not the pattern of results he had always achieved. However when you consider that three of the draws were against Scotland's Colin McNab (FIDE 2435), West Germany's Matthias Wahls (FIDE 2435) and the USA's Alex Fishbein (FIDE 2410), you begin to appreciate the quality of the event. The critical game was against Tony Kosten in Round Nine and Michael was unfortunate to be given a second successive Black and was beaten. Michael required a win in the final round to finish third, but was drawn against Chris Ward, who was sharing a flat with him and only required a draw to achieve his first IM norm and that result was duly achieved.

Michael stayed on for the weekend tournament and after conceding a draw in the first round to P. Heaven (BCF 175), he went on to win his last five games, beating Keith Arkell and Jim Plaskett in the final two rounds.

Michael was fortunate to have a third opportunity of playing Gary Kasparov in a third simultaneous event as part of the Cannes Chess Festival. The World Champion was in Cannes and he played ten opponents in different parts of the world by way of television satellite. Michael was in London, while other opponents were in Australia, Belgium, Canada, Italy, Japan, Senegal, Switzerland, the USA and the USSR. The World Champion won eight and drew one of his ten games, but lost to Michael.

Game 42   14.2.88
G.Kasparov-Adams
Satellite Simultaneous from the
Cannes Chess Festival
Bogoljubow-Indian Defence

1	d4	♘f6
2	c4	e6
3	♘f3	♗b4+
4	♘bd2	b6
5	e3	♗b7
6	♗d3	0-0
7	0-0	

Also possible is 7 a3, when White would obtain the two bishops. The text move is more solid.

7	...	d5
8	a3	♗e7

Although Black has lost time moving his bishop, White's knight has been forced to a more passive square. In this position, it would be better placed on c3.

9 b4

Also possible is 9 ♕e2 with the idea of e4.

9	...	♘bd7
10	cxd5	

It is rather early to resolve the tension in the centre. White should try to keep the option of c5 for himself. 10 ♖b1 was better.

10	...	exd5
11	♖b1	a6!

White was threatening to give me a backward pawn on c7 by playing b5.

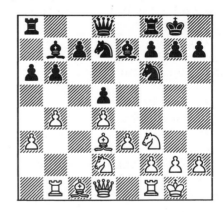

12 ♘e5

More consistent here was 12 a4, with the idea of b5. The move played, aiming for a kingside attack, is somewhat optimistic, but Black's game was comfortable in any case.

12	...	♗d6

13	f4	♞e4
14	♞xe4	dxe4
15	♞xd7	♛xd7
16	♝c4	♝e7

The bishop has been oscillating between d6 and e7 for some time, fulfilling a very useful purpose. Now it prepares ♝d5, exchanging light squared bishops and leaving the World Champion with a very bad dark squared bishop.

17	♝d2	♝d5
18	♖c1	

Better here was 18 ♝xd5 ♛xd5 19 ♛b3. When Kasparov did capture the bishop in the game, I was able to recapture with the pawn, giving me an advantage.

18	...	c6
19	♛b3	♖fc8
20	♖c2	b5
21	♝xd5	cxd5
22	♖xc8+	♖xc8
23	♖a1	

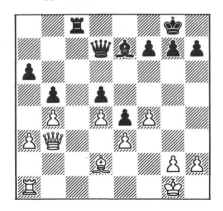

Opening the a-file was over-optimistic, whereas White should sit tight and see if Black can make any progress. Weakening the b4 pawn can only help me. White should be playing for the draw.

23	...	♖c4
24	a4	g6
25	h3	♔g7
26	axb5	axb5
27	♖a6	♝h4

I am threatening ... ♝g3, when his king would be in great danger, so the reply is forced.

28	♔h2	♛c8
29	♖a7	♛c6

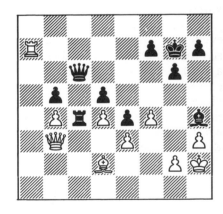

30 ♛d1

A bad mistake. Completely forced was 30 ♖a2, although I would still retain an advantage.

30	...	♖c2
31	♛g4	♝f6

32	♕d1	♖b2
33	♗e1	♕c4
34	♕g4	♕f1
35	f5	g5

35 ... h5?? would have been disastrous as then 36 ♕xg6+ would be winning for White.

36	♕g3	h5
37	♗c3	♖c2

White resigns

Although material is still equal, White's position is hopeless. 38 ♖a1 is probably the best move, but 38 ... ♕xf5 sees the first pawn

lost, while I would retain all my other advantages.

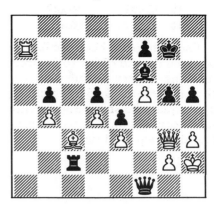

He completed a hat trick of victories at Exeter in the East Devon Open, where he defeated his main rival, Alan Ashby, in Round Four.

Unfortunately he was unable to defend his West of England title as the event coincided with the Oakham Junior International. The event was stronger than before and there were sufficient Grandmasters to make a GM norm a possibility. Unfortunately they did not perform well enough to keep up with the leaders so that neither the winner, James Howell (7½ out of 9) nor Michael, a point behind in second equal place, played sufficient GMs to qualify for a norm. Michael's best wins were against Jon Arnason (Iceland), only his second GM scalp, and Gad Rechlis (Israel).

	Game 43	31.3.88
	Adams-J.Arnason (FIDE 2510)	
	Oakham	
	Round Four	
	Ruy Lopez	

1	e4	e5
2	♘f3	♘c6
3	♗b5	a6
4	♗a4	♘f6
5	0-0	♗e7
6	♖e1	b5
7	♗b3	d6
8	c3	0-0
9	h3	♘a5
10	♗c2	c5
11	d4	♗b7
12	♘bd2	

Black's last move offered a pawn sacrifice, which, according to theory, should be accepted. By not doing so, I give my opponent a comfortable game.

12	...	cxd4
13	cxd4	♖c8
14	d5	♘h5

Black should be fine in this position, as he has improved greatly on the normal main line.

15 ♘b3

This leaves Black's knight better placed than mine on the queenside, but I had to prevent ... ♘f4.

15	...	♘c4
16	a4	♕c7
17	♗b1	g6

Better was 17 ... ♘f4. Now I have some time to unravel my pieces.

18 ♘bd2   ♖b8

This manoeuvre envisages bringing the bishop from b7 to d7, where it defends b5 and would also support an f5 advance. However the plan is far too slow. Perhaps 18 ... ♘g7 with the idea of f5 is better.

| 19 | b3 | ♘xd2 |
| 20 | ♗xd2 | ♗c8 |

He does bring his light-squared bishop to a better square but he is not able to bring his kingside

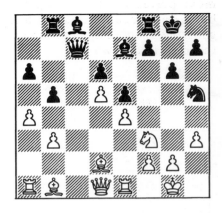

knight back into the battle. My pressure on the queenside, where I have a space advantage, is becoming unpleasant for Black.

21	axb5	axb5
22	♕c1	♕b7
23	♗e3	♖a8
24	♖xa8	♕xa8
25	♕c7	

Without making an obvious mistake, Black has drifted from a good position to a bad one. A feature of this pawn structure is that Black needs to organise counterplay on the kingside quickly or be crushed on the queenside.

| 25 | ... | ♖e8 |
| 26 | ♗d3! | |

All of my pieces are now in the game, especially my two bishops, which are very powerful, unlike their counterparts. It is noticeable that my last few moves have all come with tempi, which helps to explain why Black's position has deteriorated so quickly.

26	...	♕a6
27	♖c1	♘f6
28	♗g5	♔g7
29	♖c6	♕a1+
30	♔h2	♕d1
31	♗xf6+	♔xf6
32	♗xb5	♖d8

(see diagram)

33 ♖c3

This is a much better move than more aggressive attempts like 33 ♘xe5, as I tidy up my own

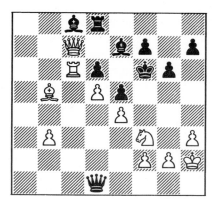

position and leave Black powerless to prevent the same idea.

33	...	g5
34	♘xg5	**Resigns**

From Oakham, Michael travelled down to London to complete a hat trick of victories in the Lloyds Bank BCF Junior Squad Under 21 event. It is easy to assume that these wins were easy to come by until you look at the players that Michael was up against. He defeated P.Georghiou (BCF 193), drew with R.Willmoth (BCF 203), then beat Graham Burgess (BCF 193), Ian Thomas (BCF 220), Michael Hennigan (BCF 210) and D.Djurović of Yugoslavia (FIDE 2230).

Game 44   10.4.88
Adams-D.Djurović (FIDE 2230)
Lloyds Bank BCF Squad Under 21
Round Six
Sicilian Defence

1	e4	c5
2	♘f3	d6
3	d4	cxd4
4	♘xd4	♘f6
5	♘c3	a6
6	♗e3	e6
7	♕d2	♗e7
8	f3	0-0
9	0-0-0	♘c6

This variation offers White good attacking chances. Najdorf players have recently shown more interest in delaying castling to speed the queenside counter attack.

| 10 | g4 | ♘xd4 |
| 11 | ♗xd4 | b5 |

Better is the immediate 11 ... ♘d7.

| 12 | g5 | ♘d7 |
| 13 | h4 | |

Better here is 13 f4, taking away the e5 square from Black's knight, although my opponent did not take advantage of my negligence. It was Black's best plan.

13	...	♖b8
14	♖g1	b4
15	♘e2	♛c7

Stronger was 15 ... ♘e5 16 ♖g3 ♘c4 17 ♛e1 e5, with reasonable counterplay.

| 16 | ♔b1 | ♗b7 |
| 17 | h5 | d5 |

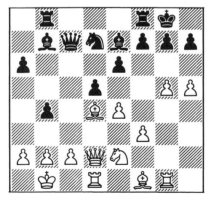

The plan of a central strike to counteract White's kingside pawn storm is often approved of in basic strategy books, but here White's attack is too strong, with well placed pieces to control the lines opened by the pawn advances.

18	g6	e5
19	gxh7+	♔xh7
20	♗h3!	

A fairly simple sacrifice to calculate, but one which has great effect. After 20 ... exd4 21 ♖xg7+ ♔xg7 22 ♖g1+, with mate in a couple of moves.

| 20 | ... | f5 |

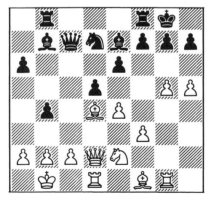

21 ♘f4!

A visually pleasing move, where I deliberately step into a fork. The move wins.

21	...	♖f6
22	♗xf5+	♖xf5
23	exf5	

Also possible was 23 ♖xg7+

♔xg7 24 ♘e6+, winning Black's
queen. My move is a more certain
route to victory, although possibly
less attractive.

23	...	♗f6
24	♘e6	♕d6
25	♗e3	♘f8
26	♗c5	**Resigns**

There followed a two month break from competitive chess, while
Michael was involved with GCSE exams. Even then he was in the public
eye, as he and Gary Lane were featured in a television documentary "To
Kill a King", which investigated whether chess was the key to understanding the brain. Children from King Charles School were also shown
in the programme, along with their headmaster.

Michael resumed his chess playing at Leeds, where the British Open
Quickplay was held. He made a tremendous start with six wins and a
draw in his first seven games, with wins against Jim Plaskett, Murray
Chandler and Glenn Flear in successive rounds. Unfortunately this was
followed by defeats against John Nunn, Mark Hebden (again!) and Keith
Arkell, so that a last round win only left him in eighth equal position.

Freed from school commitments, Michael was able to travel to
Bracknell with Chris Ward the following weekend and they shared first
equal place with four and a half points out of five in the Berkshire Open,
not surprisingly drawing their final round clash.

In his final tournament before the British Championship, he won the
Charlton event with a perfect score, defeating A.P.Lewis (BCF 207),
J.A.Johnson (BCF 193) and Peter Large (BCF 226) in the final three
rounds.

The BCF Congress was held in Blackpool and began with a quickplay
competition on the top of an open topped tram on Sunday morning,
played on portable chess sets. Michael won the event with four wins and a
draw. However his record was not so good at the open air simultaneous
that he gave and I believe he conceded lots of defeats.

He did not begin too well in the Championship, itself, drawing and
losing with White in Rounds One and Three against Angus Dunnington
and Chris Beaumont. However three successive wins enabled him to
reach what was becoming the norm – a score of four and a half out of six
at the weekend break. Michael's win with Black against Tony Kosten in
Round Six was especially pleasing.

It may have encouraged him to play in the Sunday Quickplay, which he
won for a third successive year. However the critics were able to say they

were right, when Michael lost, again with White against Stuart Conquest in Monday's game. However he really did enjoy this form of chess and he had still not reached the stage of his career where he spent time preparing for various opponents.

Another good win with Black against Keith Arkell put him back in the hunt, but despite a determined effort, he was unable to do better than draw against Murray Chandler. The same result was obtained against Niaz Murshed (Bangladesh) in the penultimate round. However a final round victory against John Pigott lifted his final score to seven and a half points to overtake his scores at Southampton and Swansea. His final position was fifth equal behind the winner, Jonathan Mestel, and Chandler, Flear and Murshed in second equal position.

Michael returned to Cornwall for a week's break before travelling to London for the Lloyds Bank Masters. If his start in the British had been disappointing, then this was nearly disastrous, with just two draws to his credit after three rounds. Two Whites had ended in a draw against S. Le Blancq and a defeat against Andrew Kinsman, while he drew with Black against Ian McKay. If he had suffered another defeat, I would have contemplated discussing a possible withdrawal to concentrate on the next tournament, but the situation never arose as he registered seven successive wins to finish first equal with Gary Lane, although Gary was awarded the title on tie-break. Michael's final three victims were J.Przewoznik (FIDE 2370) of Poland, Matthew Sadler (FIDE 2385) and Murray Chandler (FIDE 2610). If you ever made up a story like that, people would say it was too far fetched to be true!

Game 45   28.8.88
Adams-M.Sadler (FIDE 2385)
Lloyds Bank Masters
Round Nine
Sicilian Defence

1	e4	c5
2	♘f3	d6
3	d4	cxd4
4	♘xd4	♘f6
5	♘c3	a6
6	♗e3	e5
7	♘b3	

A sharper continuation than the more usual 7 ♘f3.

7	...	♗e6
8	♕d2	♗e7
9	f3	

An alternative plan in this position would be 9 f4. After the text move, both players plan to launch pawn storms against the castled kings.

9	...	0-0

10	0-0-0	b5
11	g4	b4
12	♘a4	♘c6
13	g5	♘d7
14	h4	♘a5

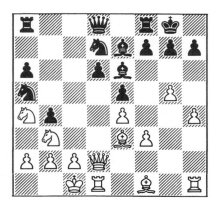

15 ♔b1

I missed my opponent's next move, after which the knight on a4 is endangered. Better was 15 ♕f2.

15	...	♘c4
16	♗xc4	♗xc4
17	♕xb4	

A regrettable necessity, but 17 ... a5 followed by ... ♗b5 was threatened.

17	...	♗e2
18	♖dg1	♗xf3
19	♖h2	d5
20	♕b7	d4

20 ... ♗xe4 21 ♘c3 and 20 ... dxe4 21 ♖d2 present no real problems for me.

21	♗c1	♖b8
22	♕c6	♕c8
23	♕xc8	♖fxc8
24	♘d2	

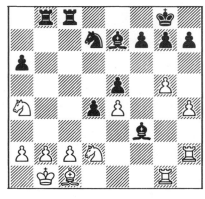

24 ... ♗xe4

This move was based on a visual error, as my opponent simply missed that my 26th move was possible. Better was 24 ... ♗h5 25 b3, when Black stands slightly better due to the advantage of the two bishops.

25	♘xe4	♖c4
26	b4	♖cxb4+

Better was 26 ... ♗xb4. Possibly my opponent was still shocked after missing the previous move.

27	♘b2	♘c5
28	c3	♖4b6
29	♘xc5	♗xc5
30	cxd4	♗xd4
31	♖d1	f5

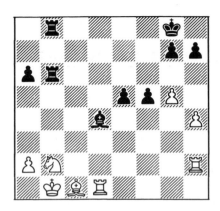

Although I am a piece for two pawns up, the tangled state of my forces and the fact that his pawns are connected and passed means that the technical problems are quite considerable.

| 32 | gxf6 | gxf6 |
| 33 | a3 | |

The first stage of my plan to break the pin on the b-file.

| 33 | ... | f5 |
| 34 | ♔a2 | f4 |

A natural looking move, but it does not turn out well. Possibly Black should have played 34 ... ♖c8 to restrict my knight.

35 ♘c4

My first conclusion was that there was no more than a draw, but after some thought, I found an unpleasant surprise to spring on my opponent on my 41st move.

35	...	♖c6
36	♖g2+	♔f8
37	♘a5	♖cb6
38	♘c4	♖c6
39	♘a5	♖cb6
40	♖c2	♖b1
41	♖xd4!	

This sacrifice leads to a technically won game, although it takes some time to achieve the full point.

41	...	exd4
42	♗xf4	♖8b5
43	a4	♖xa5
44	♔xb1	♖xa4
45	♖f2	

The fact that the h-pawn's queening square is covered by the bishop means that the exchange of rooks is not feared by White and makes the task a lot easier.

45	...	♔g7
46	♔b2	♔g6
47	♗g5	♖b4+
48	♔c2	♖b6
49	♔d3	♖d6
50	♖g2	♔h5
51	♗e7	♖d7
52	♖e2	a5
53	♖e5+	♔g4
54	♗f6	♖d6
55	♖e4+	♔h5
56	♗xd4	a4
57	♔c2	♖c6+
58	♗c3	♖a6
59	♔b2	♖a8
60	♔a3	♖a6
61	♗e1	**Resigns**

11   Grandmaster and British Champion

Having obtained a very good set of GCSE passes, Michael was due to enter the sixth form of Truro School to embark on an "A" level course studying Geography, Latin and Mathematics. Margaret and I knew that a crucial two years lay ahead for Michael and that it was not going to be easy making the correct decisions as far as school and chess were concerned. We knew that it was inevitable that some school would be missed because of chess commitments, as he had been selected to represent England at the World Junior event in Australia. We discussed the situation with Michael and together we decided that the intention would be to work hard for success at school as well as chess.

Unfortunately for the former cause, Michael was missing from school on the first day of term as he was engaged at the Nat West Young Masters All-play-All, which was a much stronger event than the previous year, with GM norms available for those scoring six points from their nine games. A first round win against Julian Hodgson gave Michael a good start, which was consolidated by a draw with Black against Daniel King. Then came the inevitable defeat with White against Mark Hebden, but Michael bounced back to defeat Tony Kosten on the following day. A quick draw against David Norwood with Black meant that three points were needed from the remaining four games if the norm was to be achieved. It was a tall order, but became more of a possibility after he had defeated Heikki Westerinen (Finland) and Colin McNab, leaving one point needed from his games with Sergey Kudrin (USA) and Ian Rogers (Australia), who were both in contention to win the tournament and were not going to do Michael any favours by agreeing quick draws. Michael had White against Kudrin first and wisely made a big effort to go for a win, knowing that he had Black in the last round. However he could make no impression on a rock solid defence and had to settle for a draw. In the final round, Michael had to employ a resourceful defence to save a difficult endgame, but eventually the GM norm was achieved and Michael became the third youngest ever to achieve the mark behind

Fischer and Kasparov. He shared first place with David Norwood, who also recorded his first GM norm, and Sergey Kudrin.

Game 46   6.9.88
Adams-H.Westerinen (FIDE 2395)
NatWest All-play-All
Round Six
Ruy Lopez

1	e4	e5
2	♘f3	♘c6
3	♗b5	a6
4	♗a4	♘f6
5	0-0	♗e7
6	♖e1	b5
7	♗b3	d6
8	c3	0-0
9	h3	♘a5
10	♗c2	c5
11	d4	♘c6

This line of the Closed Spanish does not enjoy a particularly good reputation and this game does nothing to alter that reputation.

| 12 | d5 | ♘a7 |
| 13 | ♘bd2 | |

Possibly even stronger was 13 b3 to limit Black's expansion on the queenside, when White, because of his space advantage, would find it easier to transfer his pieces to the other side of the board.

13	...	c4
14	♘f1	a5
15	♘e3	♕c7

| 16 | ♕e2 | ♘h5 |

Black would do better with a simple move like 16 ... ♗d7. The move played is rather more ambitious than his position can support.

17 a4!

I was not worried by 17 ... ♘f4, which is not a serious problem. I take the opportunity to break down Black's queenside structure. His main problem is the knight on a7 that rarely comes into play. As the game develops, this advantage becomes more relevant.

17	...	♘f4
18	♕f1	♗d7
19	♘f5!	

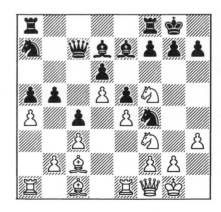

Now Black has great problems, as his knight on f4 is going to be taken and then I will have the very powerful d4 square for my knights. If 19 ... ♗xf5 20 exf5 ♘xd5 21 ♗c4 wins material.

19	...	♖ae8
20	axb5	♗xb5
21	♗xf4	exf4
22	♗a4	

My last dormant piece is exchanged and now Black's many weak pawns are exposed. As pieces are exchanged, the weakness of the knight on a7 becomes more pronounced. After this move, Black is probably lost.

22	...	♖b8
23	♗xb5	♖xb5
24	♘xe7+	♕xe7
25	♕xc4	

The move wins a pawn and retains White's positional advantages.

25	...	♖fb8
26	e5	♖xb2
27	♕xf4	♘b5

No better was 27 ... dxe5 28 ♘xe5 ♕b7 (28 ... ♕c7 29 d6) 29

c4.

| 28 | c4 | ♖b4 |
| 29 | ♖xa5 | ♕c7 |

30 ♖xb5!

A simple but pleasing way to end the game. This exchange sacrifice wins on the spot.

30	...	♖8xb5
31	exd6	♕d8
32	d7	**Resigns**

If 32 ... ♕xd7, simplest is 33 ♕f5, followed by capturing the rook on b5, as the queen is now unpinned.

We had not anticipated a triumph like this and when Michael did take his place at his school desk four days after the start of term, I have the feeling that whatever his mind was telling him to do, his heart was far more interested in a chess career than an academic one and the GM norm was conclusive proof that he could be successful in his chosen career.

Within a fortnight, he was setting off to Australia for the World Junior event with David Norwood. Michael's result at the World Junior was a great disappointment for him and cannot easily be explained. He made a good start, winning his first two games and then drawing with Ivanchuk (USSR), who was the highest rated player in the tournament, and Zsuzsa Polgar (Hungary). In Round Five, Oakham 1986 repeated itself with Michael turning down Pavel Blatny's draw offer and going on to lose. The same thing happened in the next round against Weiguo Lin (China) and suddenly he was back to fifty per cent. From then on, he tried too hard and fine wins were littered with disappointing defeats as he finally finished with seven out of thirteen, with David Norwood half a point further behind. Michael did win the best game prize for his win against the Spaniard, Luis Comas, but that was small compensation for the disappointing result.

We began to wonder if Michael did have a future in chess after this result. It was quite a distressing time for Margaret and myself, as you feel so helpless being so far away and the only information that you are receiving is the results. However on the few occasions that Michael has experienced setbacks, he has always bounced back with a fine performance and so it was now.

About a fortnight after he returned to England, he was one of eight players invited to play in the James Capel Speed Chess Challenge, a knock-out event filmed for Thames TV. Players were allowed 25 minutes for their games, with this being reduced to five minutes for replays. Michael faced Murray Chandler in his first match and managed to defend doggedly to hold the draw and then outplay his opponent in the replay. He also beat Jon Speelman in the semi final in the second game after the first had been drawn. Michael had probably had the best of the drawn game, but was losing the replay, until inaccuracies swung it his way in the short thinking time allowed to players in these games. In the final, Michael faced Nigel Short and they proceeded to draw five games before Michael succumbed.

Like many other players, Michael travelled to Thessaloniki to watch some of the Olympiad and play in the Open that was held nearby. He shared first place with eight others, including English players Keith Arkell, Stuart Conquest, Glenn Flear, Julian Hodgson and Peter Wells, who was the only player to defeat Michael.

On a rest day, there was a quickplay competition, which some of the Olympiad players took part in and Michael led into the last double round of the competition, but unfortunately was paired with Mark Hebden and lost both games.

In an effort to broaden his chess experience, Michael joined Clichy, a Paris side, to play in the French League, hoping that a successful season with the right opponents might bring another GM norm. He had the successful season, winning eight, drawing one and losing two of his games, as he helped Clichy win the French Championship. However he did not play enough GMs to register a norm. His defeats were at the hands of Joel Lautier, the new World Junior Champion, and Mark Hebden.

In the Christmas holidays, Michael decided to play in the European Junior at Arnhem. It was not an easy decision to make, as he could have stayed in England and been home for Christmas before travelling to Hastings for the Challengers. If we had our time again, that is what we would do. However I encouraged Michael to play at Arnhem to dispel the myth that he could not play junior tournaments. Instead his result reinforced this view as he finished with a fifty per cent score, despite being the third seed.

Michael's next overseas appearance was at the Cannes Chess Festival, where "The Generation Tournament" was held. The young included Lautier, Anand, Renet, Miralles and Michael against a more experienced generation of Tal, Spassky, Larsen, Andersson and Csom. The youngsters played each senior twice, with the GM mark at five and a half points. Michael was well on target at half way with four draws and a win against Csom. Unfortunately Tal had to withdraw through ill health at this point and Tony Miles took his place. This had the effect of increasing the GM mark to six points. Nevertheless a win against Larsen and draws against Andersson and Csom meant that Michael only required a point from his final two games. When he reached a favourable position against Spassky, he felt obliged to go for a win but it rebounded on him and he lost. The ironic thing was that if Tal had still been in the tournament, a draw could have easily been achieved and a second norm obtained. As it was, he had to go for a win with Black in his game against Miles and was hopelessly outplayed.

By this time, his "A" levels had come second to chess. Latin had been dropped and much crucial work was missed, although he continued to attend school when he was home and also to represent the school at chess. With Matthew Piper getting stronger all the time, it was very rare for the school team not to be two up from their top board results and they enjoyed a fine run in "The Times" tournament, reaching the final stages.

However only half a point from the bottom four boards meant that they lost 2½-3½ to Manchester Grammar School in the semi-final, although they did finish third when they defeated Antrim Grammar School 4-2.

Michael stayed on in Paris after the last league game to play in the Paris Open. He won this event outright with a score of eight out of nine, only conceding draws to Tony Kosten and D.Petrović (Yugoslavia).

Now that he was not so concerned about school attendance, Michael played in several weekend tournaments, winning for a fourth successive year at Exeter with a maximum score. He performed the same feat at Hitchin and only dropped a half point at Blackpool and Folkestone over five and seven rounds to earn several Leigh Grand Prix points. Without going out of his way, he had finished second in the 1988 Grand Prix, which had earned him a 40 point bonus for 1989 and it seemed sensible to attempt to accumulate sufficient points to see if he could go one better this year. However it was not always plain sailing and defeats by Keith Arkell at Chester and Paul Littlewood at St. Albans meant that a whole weekend's work brought ño tangible reward.

Michael was given another chance of a GM norm at Park Hall, another all-play-all event with the norm mark at six out of nine. Michael began well with two wins with White against Nigel Davies and Brett Lund, sandwiching a draw with Black against Patrick Wolff (USA). He then safely achieved draws against Ivan Sokolov (Yugoslavia) and Michael Wilder (USA), before defeating Mihai Suba and Jonathan Levitt, leaving just half a point required from his remaining games.

Game 47   24.6.89
Adams-J.Levitt (FIDE 2495)
Park Hall All-Play-All
Round Seven
French Defence

1	e4	e6
2	d4	d5
3	♘d2	c5
4	exd5	♕xd5
5	♘gf3	cxd4
6	♗c4	♕d6
7	0-0	♘f6

8	♘b3	♘c6
9	♘bxd4	♘xd4
10	♘xd4	a6
11	♖e1	

It is fairly easy to predict that Jon Levitt will defend this opening variation. My plan was to follow an earlier game, which Speelman won against Nogueiras.

11	...	♕c7
12	♕e2	♗c5
13	c3	

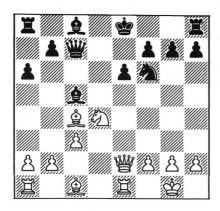

13   ...   b5!

An improvement on the afore-mentioned game. Nogueiras played 13 ... ♗xd4 14 cxd4 0-0 immediately, which gave White a comfortable edge after 15 ♗g5. The game move forced me to commit my light squared bishop immediately and allowed Black equality.

14	♗d3	♗xd4
15	cxd4	0-0
16	♗g5	♘d5
17	♖ac1	♕d6
18	♕h5	f5
19	♕h4	♗b7
20	♖e5	h6
21	♗d2	♖f6
22	a3	♖d8
23	♖ce1	♘b6

With this unfortunate blunder, Black offered a draw. After the better 23 ... ♖d7, the game would remain approximately equal. Now I win by force, albeit in rather a complicated manner.

24   ♖xe6   ♕xd4

The alternative 24 ... ♖xe6 25 ♖xe6 ♕xe6 26 ♕xd8+ ♔h7 27 f3 does not hold out much hope for Black either.

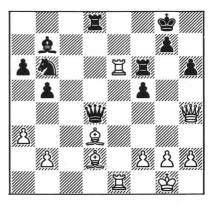

25   ♖e8+!   ♔h7

Of course not 25 ... ♖xe8 26 ♕xd4, while 25 ... ♔f7 26 ♕h5+ g6 27 ♖1e7 mate does not help either.

26	♕xd4	♖xd4
27	♗c3!	

The point of the combination. Although Black temporarily obtains two pieces for a rook, I can then pick up a piece.

27	...	♖xd3
28	♗xf6	gxf6
29	♖8e7+	♔g6
30	♖xb7	♘c4
31	♖a7	a5
32	f4!	

A good move. Although I am winning in any event, fixing his pawns, and thereby putting his king in danger, is the safest way to victory.

| 32 | ... | a4 |
| 33 | ♖a6 | ♘d2 |

If 33 ... ♘xb2 34 ♖ee6 is very unpleasant.

34	♖e2	♘e4
35	g3	♖b3
36	♔g2	♖d3
37	♖b6	♖b3
38	♖c2	♔h5

| 39 | ♔h3 | ♔g6 |
| 40 | ♔h4 | h5 |

A neat example of *zugzwang*, where I wanted Black to play ... h5 to take away the escape square from his king. As neither of Black's other pieces can move without loss of material, ... h5 is now forced as 40 ... ♔g7 41 ♖c7+ ♔g6 42 ♖bb7 is fatal.

| 41 | ♔h3 | ♔h6 |
| 42 | ♖c7 | **Resigns** |

Now if 42 ... ♖xb2 43 ♖bb7 leads to mate.

The norm was duly achieved in Round Eight, when he drew with Jon Tisdall (Norway).

Game 48　　　25.6.89
J.Tisdall (FIDE 2460)-**Adams**
Park Hall All-play-All
Round Eight
French Defence

1	e4	e6
2	d4	d5
3	♘d2	♘f6
4	e5	♘fd7
5	c3	c5
6	f4	♘c6
7	♘df3	♕b6
8	h4	

This is the most recent idea in this line, replacing the old 8 g3 as the most critical continuation. In this variation, White aims to set up a large centre but allows Black compensation due to the exposed position of his king.

| 8 | ... | f6 |
| 9 | ♗d3 | |

More accurate was 9 a3. After the move played, the displacement of White's king will allow Black to obtain reasonable counter-chances.

9	...	cxd4
10	cxd4	♗b4+
11	♔e2	♗e7
12	a3	0-0
13	b4	

White is taking too many liberties in this variation. He should have paid more attention to safety by means of 13 ♔e1.

13	...	fxe5
14	fxe5	♘xd4+!

A fairly common idea in this variation but here it is more effective than usual due to the weakened g4 square and White's lack of development.

15	♘xd4	♘xe5
16	♗g5	♗f6
17	♗xf6	♖xf6
18	♘h3	♘g4
19	♕g1	e5

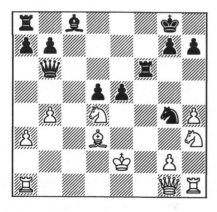

20 ♘f3!

Although this allows me to regain my piece, White has defended in the most accurate way. Although ·the ending should be lost for White, there are several technical problems to overcome.

20	...	e4
21	♕xb6	axb6
22	♘d4	exd3+
23	♔xd3	♘e5+
24	♔c3	♗xh3
25	♖xh3	♖f4

Even now, I have not decided which is the most precise way of exploiting the pawn advantage. Certainly this move was not to blame.

26	♘b5	♖g4

Probably better was 26 ... d4+ 27 ♔b3 ♖e4. After the text move, my knight is driven away from the strong e5 square.

27	♖e3	♘c6
28	♖d1	d4+
29	♘xd4	

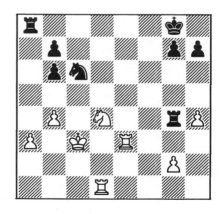

29	...	♖xa3+

If 29 ... ♘xd4 30 ♖xd4 ♖xa3+ 31 ♔c4 ♖xd4+ 32 ♔xd4 ♖xe3 33

♔xe3, the arising pawn ending is a draw. Hence I decided to take on a3 immediately. The fact that my technique has not been the best can be clearly seen from the way in which my d-pawn was lost.

| 30 | ♘b3 | ♖a8 |

My original intention was 30 ... ♖xb4. However I was unconvinced that I would have real winning chances in the variation 31 ♖d8+ ♘xd8 32 ♔xb4. After the move played, White probably has suffi-

cient to hold the draw, but accurate play is required to do so.

31	b5	♘a5
32	♘xa5	bxa5
33	♖d7	b6
34	♖b7	a4
½-½		

I am still better in the final position, but as White will shortly acquire a passed pawn of his own, the position is no longer so risk-free and I was anxious to register my second GM norm.

In the final round, he drew with Julian Hodgson to clinch outright victory, undoubtedly his best tournament result so far.

Michael then crossed the Pennines for the NatWest British Speed Championships at Leeds, where he achieved another noteworthy result, finishing third equal with Ivan Sokolov, behind John Nunn and Peter Wells. His only defeat was at the hands of Sokolov, who had offered a draw at one stage only for Michael to decline it, as both players were under the mistaken impression that Michael was winning. His draws were against John Nunn, Peter Wells and Tony Kosten, while he included Michael Wilder, Stuart Conquest, Paul Motwani and a Fidelity computer among his victims.

He was fortunate to have a chance to complete his GM title requirements almost immediately. It was not like the long wait for the third IM norm. The chance came at the Icklicki Masters tournament, where two teams of nine players opposed each other. The GM mark was seven out of nine and this obviously allowed little margin for error. A draw against Ali Mortazavi did not appear the best of starts, but Ali is a dangerous player, especially in the early rounds of a tournament. However the wins began to appear and he won his next three games.

Game 49   14.7.89   Icklicki Masters, Round Four
M.Dutreeuw (FIDE 2400)-Adams   *French Defence*

1	e4	e6
2	d4	d5
3	♘c3	♗b4
4	e5	♘e7
5	♗d2	

A rather unusual variation of the French Defence. More critical was 5 ♕g4.

5	...	c5
6	♘b5	♗xd2+
7	♕xd2	0-0
8	c3	

Probably better was 8 dxc5, when the White knight is able to retreat to d4.

8	...	♗d7

More accurate than 8 ... ♘bc6 as this move gains a tempo on the knight on b5.

9	♘f3	♕b6
10	♘a3	

10 ♘d6 would not help White as its exposed position would be easily exploited by a central counter attack by means of a later ... f6.

10	...	♘bc6
11	♗e2	cxd4
12	cxd4	♘f5
13	0-0-0	

More natural was 13 ♖d1 but it is strongly answered by 13 ... ♘b4.

13	...	f6
14	exf6	♖xf6

15	♔b1	

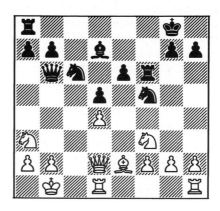

15	...	♗e8!

I take the opportunity to bring my problem piece, the light squared bishop, to a more effective post. Black has a very pleasant position.

16	h4	♗h5
17	♘c2	a5
18	♕g5	

This was not a move that my opponent wanted to play. However none of the alternatives look attractive, although 18 ♘e5 was worthy of consideration.

18	...	♗xf3
19	♗xf3	a4

19 ... ♘cxd4 20 ♘xd4 ♘xd4 21 ♕e3 is obviously no good for Black, but my powerfully placed pieces together with White's weakened king position mean that I am clearly better.

20	♕d2

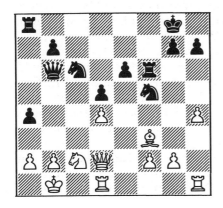

20	...	a3!

The beginning of a piece of accurate calculation. At this stage I saw until the end of the game.

21	b3	♖a4
22	♔a1	♘fxd4
23	♘xd4	♖xd4
24	♕e3	♖xd1+
25	♖xd1	♕xe3
26	fxe3	♘e5

27	♖f1	♘xf3
28	gxf3	

The pawn ending arising after 28 ♖xf3 ♖xf3 29 gxf3 ♔f7 is also hopeless for White.

28	...	♖g6
29	♔b1	♖g2

White resigns

At first it may appear that the resignation is a trifle premature, but with my rook on the seventh rank, all I have to do is play ♖b2+ and force his king into the corner and pick off the White pawns at will.

This was a good, solid performance. When playing lower rated opponents in events where a GM norm is a possibility, it is tempting to overpress and to become over-ambitious. In this game, I played sensibly throughout and kept the pressure on my opponent without forcing matters unduly.

The next two games were drawn against R.Polaczek (Belgium) and Julian Hodgson, leaving two and a half points needed from his last three games. Michael played the Bishop's Opening to prevent D.Pergericht (Belgium) using the Petroff Defence and this paid off to give him one win and in the following round he deliberately chose an unusual opening system against M.Schrentzel (Israel), leading to an unclear position where Michael calculated that his superior rating should prove decisive and that indeed is what happened. Thus a quick draw against M.Matulović (Yugoslavia) enabled him to join the ranks of the grandmasters as the third youngest behind Fischer and Kasparov and the youngest contemporary grandmaster.

Ten days afterwards, the British Championships began at the Plymouth Guildhall. For several years, it was thought that they would be held there to celebrate the centenary of the Plymouth Chess Club and just as little boys dream of scoring winning goals at Wembley and centuries at Lords, so I had always thought that Michael might win the British Championship there. After all, it was as near to our native Cornwall that the event would ever come and it was in the same building where he had defeated his first grandmaster and won two tournaments while remaining unbeaten. As if that was not enough, the last round would coincide with the writer's fiftieth birthday and what greater birthday present could there be than your son winning the British Chess Championship.

Were these omens or just childish dreams? The first week did not answer the question. The weekend score was again four and a half, three White wins and three Black draws. Only Jim Plaskett and David Norwood lay ahead on five.

The Sunday Quickplay was given a miss, although it was not clear whether this indicated a more serious approach or whether it was becoming increasingly difficult to get up for morning rounds. Whichever it was, it did not seem to do a lot of good, as he drew with Neil McDonald and only avoided defeat by accurate defence in a difficult ending. When his run of White successes came to an end and he could only draw with Jonathan Levitt, his chances seemed to have disappeared as five players were ahead of him with only three rounds to go.

In Round Nine, Michael had a strange game with Keith Arkell, where he was clearly worse from the opening but then managed to prove that his Black pawn advance was more effective than his opponent's, although it had not seemed like that to observers. Results in other games helped Michael's cause and now only Jim Plaskett lay ahead and Michael was paired with him in the next round.

Game 50   10.8.89
J.Plaskett (FIDE 2460)-Adams
British Championship
Round Ten
English Opening

1	♘f3	♘f6	
2	d4	e6	
3	g3	b6	
4	♗g2	♗b7	
5	0-0	c5	
6	c4	cxd4	
7	♕xd4	♗e7	
8	♘c3	d6	
9	♖d1		

A standard hedgehog position has arisen. At this stage I must be careful with the move order and my next move, preventing the possibility of ♘b5, is the most accurate, after which the game is destined to take a quiet path for some time to come.

9	...	a6
10	e4	♘bd7
11	♕e3	♕c7
12	b3	0-0
13	♗b2	♖ac8
14	♘d4	♖fe8
15	♖ac1	

My opponent has problems in selecting the best squares for his rooks in this game. To an extent, this is not important as the closed nature of the game means that both sides have time to position their pieces ideally. In this slow manoeuvring type of game, I felt that I would be happier than my opponent. Black's game is the easier to play as I had the clear-cut plan of redeploying my black squared bishop.

15	...	♗f8
16	h3	♕b8
17	♖e1	g6
18	♖cd1	♗g7
19	f4	

This move, which inevitably results in the opening of the game, must be considered a mistake, as my forces were better placed than his. He should have continued manoeuvring with a move such as 19 ♕d2. In any case, my position is entirely successful and this was

the reason for my opponent deciding on direct action.

19	...	e5
20	fxe5	♘xe5
21	♖f1	♗c6

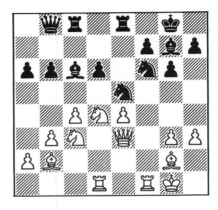

This move was played with the idea of ... b5. It should be noted that although White can capture the bishop on c6, he is obviously loath to do so, due to its ineffectual counterpart on g2.

22	a4	♗a8
23	♖f2	♘fd7
24	♖df1	

The fact that this move is retracted immediately shows that it must be a mistake. I am standing better in any event. Correct is 24 ♘d5, when 24 ... ♘c5 could not be played because of 25 ♘f6+.

24	...	♘c5
25	♖d1	

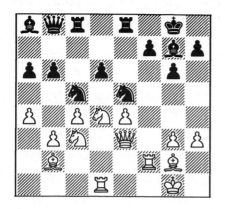

25 ...   ♘xb3

This simple, but effective, tactic allows me to make a decisive material gain. However it is easier to criticise White's last move than to suggest a constructive alternative.

26	♘xb3	♘xc4
27	♕f3	♘xb2
28	♕xf7+	♔h8
29	♖xb2	

(see diagram)

29 ...   ♖c7

The obvious 29 ... ♖xc3 was more tempting, but this accurate

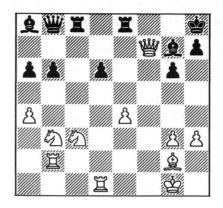

move driving White's queen from its advanced post is more effective. Although I am only one pawn up, my incredibly powerful black square bishop makes it difficult for White to put up much resistance, particularly taking into account his time trouble.

30	♕f2	♖xc3
31	♘d2	♖f8
32	♕e1	♗d4+
33	♔h1	♖e3
34	♕g1	♖d3

The double attack against White's rook and queen decides the game.

White resigns

With David Norwood defeating Julian Hodgson and joining Michael as co-leader, all that was needed was for the two friends to agree a quick draw and they would be assured of a share of first prize. Unfortunately they had already played a draw in Round Five, so we awaited the pairings with some trepidation. Murray Chandler, Daniel King and Mark Hebden were the possibilities. Needless to say there was one of these that Michael did not want to play and he felt quite relieved when he was paired with Murray Chandler.

David Norwood was paired with Mark Hebden and they quickly drew their game, thus giving David his final qualification for the GM title. Thus everything rested on Michael's game. He offered one draw, but his opponent needed a win to overhaul Michael and finish first equal and the offer was declined. As the game developed, Michael's position became stronger and stronger until he gained a material advantage and was clearly winning. His opponent fought on doggedly to take the game into an adjournment session.

I know how nervous I was feeling but Michael remained absolutely calm. I am not sure what Margaret felt waiting at home. We did ring her during the adjournment but only to say that Michael was still playing, not daring to mention that he was winning. However five minutes after the resumption, I was ringing her again to tell her that our son was the new British Champion, the youngest ever at seventeen. It was lovely that a lot of Michael's friends could be present during the last round and share the joy of Michael's triumph.

All that I could do was to think back through the last ten years and to recall all the encouragement that Michael had been given by many kind people and wish that they also could have been present.

There was another thing that I remembered and that was my advice to my son, perhaps thirteen years earlier – "You are too young to play chess. Chess is a game for grown-ups. Perhaps when you are eighteen, you might learn to play chess." Michael was still only seventeen and already he was a Grandmaster and British Champion.

Michael Adams (b. 17.11.71): Chess Career Record

Date	Tournament	P'f'mance	Score	Position
11/79	Cornwall U-10		9½/10	1/109
02/80	Cornwall U-13		5½/7	5=/58
02/80	Plymouth U-14 Quickplay		5½/9	13=/64
03/80	BCF Squad U-12	112	3½/7	46/120
03/80	Cornwall U-125	95	2½/5	
05/80	Cornwall Lightning		4/6	4=/24
06/80	Manor Tyres U-120	112	3½/5	11=/87
07/80	Holsworthy Quickplay		5/9	20=/60
79-80	Cornwall League W4 D0 L0	130		
10/80	Woolacombe U-131	103	3/5	13=/42
10/80	Barnstaple U-141	121	3/5	10=/34
11/80	Cornwall U-9		10/10	1/70
11/80	Torbay U-125	105	3/5	15=/67
12/80	Islington U-120	102	3/6	46=/120
12/80	Devon Open U-11		6½/7	1=/120
12/80	Plymouth U-115	108	3½/5	4=/34
01/81	Cornwall U-125	132	4½/5	1/32
01/81	Cornwall U-13		6½/7	1=/88
02/81	Cornwall U-15		4/5	1=
02/81	Cornwall U-18	140	4½/5	1/10
02/81	Plymouth U-14 Quickplay		7½/9	2/80
03/81	BCF Squad U-12	149	5/7	6=/110
04/81	BCF Squad U-14	134	3½/6	20=/85
04/81	Torridge U-135	149	4½/5	2=/64
05/81	WECU U-15	115	3½/5	4=/20
05/81	Elstre & B. U-130	154	4/5	4=/98
05/81	Manor Tyres U-120	103	3/5	
07/81	Holsworthy Quickplay		5½/9	14=/64
08/81	British U-11	131	5½/7	2=/31
08/81	Weymouth Reserves	124	3½/6	10=/34
80-81	Cornwall League W3 D3 L4	112		
80-81	County matches W0 D2 L1	136		
10/81	Woolacombe U-131	123	3½/5	7=/58
10/81	Barnstaple U-141	144	4½/5	6=/54
11/81	Cornwall U-10		7/7	1
11/81	Torbay U-155	166	3½/5	8=
11/81	Plymouth U-14 Quickplay		5½/6	1=/82
12/81	Devon Open U-11		5½/6	1=
12/81	Plymouth U-150	158	4½/6	1=

01/82	Cornwall U-13		7/7	1/97
02/82	Plymouth Open Quickplay		4/6	10=/78
03/82	Cornwall U-15		5/5	1/35
03/82	East Devon U-156	150	4/5	3=
03/82	BCF Squad U-12	149	6½/7	1=/87
04/82	Cornwall Championship	180	3½/5	2=/16
04/82	BCF Squad U-14	162	4½/6	2=/77
04/82	Taw U-200	139	2/6	
05/82	Cornwall Lightning		5½/7	2=
05/82	Cotwold U-155	160	4/6	6=
06/82	Manor Tyres U-160	176	4/5	2=
07/82	Holsworthy Quickplay		6/9	4=
08/82	British U-11	160	8/8	1/58
08/82	BCF Squad U-14 Quickplay	167	6/7	1=
81-82	Cornwall League W7 D6 L2	152		
81-82	County match W0 D1 L0	161		
10/82	Golden Coast U-176	166	3/5	5=/26
10/82	Barnstaple U-141 (1981 grade)	165	4½/5	2
10/82	Plymouth Open Quickplay		4/6	4=
10/82	North London U-170	179	4½/5	7=/150
11/82	Cornwall U-18		4/5	2=/39
11/82	Cornwall U-11		7/7	1/92
11/82	Torbay U-155	155	3/5	16=/53
12/82	Devon Open U-11		5/5	1
12/82	Plymouth Open	158	3½/6	7=/22
01/83	Plymouth Junior International		3½/7	10=/20
01/83	Cornwall Championship	181	4/5	1=/24
02/83	Plymouth Open Quickplay		4½/6	4=
02/83	Cornwall U-13		7/7	1/105
02/83	City U-170	156	3½/6	
03/83	Palace Quickplay		4½/7	
03/83	Cornwall U-15		6/6	1/63
03/83	East Devon Open	180	3/5	9=
03/83	Cornwall Lightning		5½/6	1
03/83	Teignmouth Quickplay		5/6	1=
04/83	West of England Championship	179	3½/7	12=/30
04/83	BCF Squad U-14	175	4½/6	3=
04/83	Taw U-200	157	2½/5	
05/83	Cotswold U-176	117	2/6	
07/83	Holsworthy Quickplay		5½/9	
07/83	Southampton Quickplay Major		7/11	10=/53
08/83	British U-14	168	8½/11	2
08/83	British Sunday Quickplay		5/7	
82-83	Cornwall League W11 D3 L2	173		
82-83	County matches W1 D2 L1	175		
09/83	BCF Squad U-14 Quickplay		7½/10	2=/60
10/83	Golden Coast U-181	191	4/5	1=/24
10/83	Barnstaple Open	186	2/5	
10/83	Cornwall U-18		5/5	1/34
11/83	Torbay Open	166	2/5	
12/83	Cornwall Quickplay		5½/6	1
12/83	Evening Standard U-14	165	6½/8	2

01/84	Plymouth Junior International		6/9	3
01/84	Cornwall Championship		4½/5	1/22
01/84	Cornwall U-13		7/7	1
01/84	British Lightning		6/9	3=/24
02/84	ARC Young Masters	204	3/6	
03/84	Plymouth Open Quickplay		4½/6	3=
03/84	Cornwall U-15		6½/7	1
03/84	Cornwall Quickplay		8½/9	1
03/84	East Devon Open	201	3/5	
04/84	BCF Squad U-18	183	3½/6	
04/84	West of England Championship	215	5/7	3=
05/84	Barnstaple Quickplay		5½/6	1=
05/84	Cotswold Open		3½/6	
07/84	WECU U-18	170	3½/5	
07/84	Holsworthy Quickplay		7/9	1/46
08/84	BCF Major Open	187	6/11	
08/84	BCF Sunday Quickplay		3/7	
08/84	BCF Squad U-21 Quickplay		6½/10	6=/55
08/84	Lloyds Bank Masters	229	5½/9	
83-84	Cornwall League W15 D1 L1	190		
83-84	County matches W3 D2 L0	215		
09/84	Paignton Open	194	4/7	10=/37
10/84	Cornwall U-18		5½/6	1
10/84	Chequers Rating	227	6½/9	2
11/84	Cornwall Quickplay		5½/6	1
11/84	Torbay Open	212	4/5	1=
12/84	Plymouth Open	201	4/6	
01/85	Plymouth Junior International		5½/9	5/18
01/85	Cornwall U-13		6½/7	1=
03/85	Cornwall Lightning		8½/9	1
03/85	East Devon Open	206	4/5	2=
03/85	Teignmouth Quickplay		5/6	3=
04/85	West of England Championship	214	5/7	2=/30
04/85	BCF Squad U-18	209	4½/6	1=
05/85	Jersey Open	180	4½/9	
05/85	Cotswold Open	209	4½/6	
07/85	WECU U-18		4½/5	1
07/85	Glorney Cup	219	4½/5	
07/85	B.R. Lightning		10½/13	2/56
08/85	British Championship	204	5/11	44=/76
08/85	BCF Sunday Quickplay		5/7	
08/85	BCF Squad U-21 Quickplay		7½/10	3/56
08/85	Lloyds Bank Masters	202	5/9	44/159
84-85	Cornwall League W11 D1 L1	206		
84-85	County matches W2 D1 L1	207		
09/85	Paignton Open	221	5½/7	1=/40
10/85	Hexagon Open	229	4½/5	1/24
11/85	Cornwall U-18		6/6	1
11/85	Cornwall Quickplay		5½/6	1=/54
11/85	Torbay Open	199	3/5	
12/85	Ilya Gurevich match	212	3/6	

01/86	Cornwall Championship		5/6	1/26
03/86	Cornwall Lightning		9/9	1
03/86	Cornwall U-15		6/6	1/42
03/86	East Devon Open	223	4½/5	1
03/86	West of England Championship	243	6½/7	1/32
04/86	Oakham Junior International	203	3½/9	33=/42
04/86	BCF Squad U-21	237	5½/6	1/23
05/86	Cotswold Open	221	5/6	1=
05/86	Cornwall U-15		6/6	1/42
06/86	British Quickplay		6½/11	
07/86	East Glamorgan Open	220	4/5	2=
07/86	Glorney Cup	226	4½/5	
08/86	British Championship	244	7/11	6=/62
08/86	BCF Sunday Quickplay		7/7	1
08/86	BCF Squad U-21 Quickplay		9½/10	1/56
08/86	Lloyds Bank Masters	232	5½/9	27=/189
85-86	Cornwall League W19 D1 L0	220		
85-86	County matches W3 D0 L1	219		
09/86	British Isles Open	209	4/6	
10/86	Hexagon Open	232	4½/5	1/24
11/86	Cornwall U-18		6/6	1/34
11/86	Torbay Open	212	4/5	2
11/86	Cornwall Quickplay		6/6	1/46
12/86	London U-21	206	4½/7	
01/87	Cornwall Championship		5½/6	1/22
02/87	ARC Young Masters	221	4½/6	5=/83
03/87	Cornwall Lightning		9/9	1/46
03/87	East Devon Open	242	5/5	1=/60
03/87	Teignmouth Quickplay		6/6	1
04/87	BCF Squad U-21	227	5/6	1
04/87	West of England Championship	219	5½/7	1/24
05/87	World U-16		9/11	2/45
06/87	Charlton Open	228	5/6	2=
07/87	BCF U-21 Blitz		23½/30	1=
07/87	Glorney Cup	222	3½/4	
08/87	British Championship	242	7/11	6=/58
08/87	BCF Sunday Quickplay		6/7	1/48
08/87	BIS Speed Qualifier		5½/7	5=/98
08/87	Lloyds Bank Masters	229	7/10	7=/187
86-87	Cornwall League W15 D2 L0	230		
86-87	County matches W5 D1 L0	232		
09/87	British Isles Open	231	5/6	1=
10/87	NatWest All-Play-All	238	6½/9	2=
10/87	Cornwall Lightning		9/9	1/38
11/87	Cornwall U-18		6/6	1
11/87	Torbay Open	238	4½/6	1=
12/87	Islington Open	249	5/6	3=/88
01/88	Hastings Challengers	231	6½/10	8=/77
01/88	Hastings Weekend Open	243	5½/6	1/52
02/88	East Devon Open	230	4½/5	1
03/88	Oakham Junior International	246	6½/9	2=/52

04/88	BCF U-21 Squad	246	5½/6	1/35
05/88	Cornwall Quickplay		6/6	1/30
06/88	British Open Quickplay		7½/11	8=/106
06/88	Berkshire Open	235	4½/5	1=
07/88	Charlton Open	249	6/6	1
08/88	British Championship	243	7½/11	5=/70
08/88	BCF Sunday Quickplay		6/6	1/74
08/88	Lloyds Bank Masters	242	8/10	1=/160
87-88	Cornwall League W13 D1 L0			
87-88	County match W1 D0 L0			
09/88	NatWest All-Play-All	254	6/9	1=
09/88	Barbican Open	229	4½/6	5=
10/88	World Junior		7/13	18
10/88	Hakoah International		6½/9	6=
10/88	North London Open	233	4½/6	2=
11/88	Cornwall U-18		4½/6	2=
11/88	Thessaloniki Open		7/9	1=
12/88	European Junior		6½/13	13=/32
01/89	Cornwall Championship		5/6	1
02/89	"Generation" Challenge	249	5/10	5=/10
03/89	East Devon Open		5/5	1
03/89	Blackpool Open	240	4½/5	1=
03/89	Folkestone Open		6½/7	1
04/89	Cornwall Quickplay		6/6	1
04/89	St Albans Open	231	3½/5	
04/89	Chester Open	238	4/5	
05/89	Paris Open		8/9	1
05/89	Watson Farley Williams All-Play-All	237	6½/13	6=/14
06/89	Park Hall All-Play-All	258	6½/9	1
07/89	British Open Quickplay		8½/11	3=/138
07/89	Hitchin Open		5/5	1
07/89	Icklicki Masters All-Play-All	253	7/9	1
08/89	British Championship	255	8½/11	1/78
08/89	Lloyds Bank Masters		7/10	
88-89	Cornwall League W6 D0 L0			
88-89	French League	249	8½/11	
09/89	NatWest All-Play-All	245	5½/9	2=/10
09/89	Ostend Open		7/9	2=
10/89	Plymouth Quickplay		8½/10	1
10/89	Hitchin Open	243	4½/5	1=
11/89	World Team	236	2½/5	
11/89	Young England v. Polgars		4½/6	
11/89	European Team	218	1½/6	
12/89	European Speed		Finalist	
12/89	GMA Open	251	5½/9	
01/90	Hastings Premier	243	6/14	8/8
02/90	Cannes Open		6½/9	
03/90	Visa match	265	4/6	
03/90	Oakham Junior International	250	6/9	6=
04/90	Manchester All-Play-All	251	7/9	2/12

05/90	Watson Farley Williams All-Play-All	246		5=/14
05/90	British Zonal	253	7½/10	2=/12
06/90	GMA Quickplay		7½/13	
06/90	British Isles Open		3½/5	
07/90	Interzonal	250	7/13	
08/90	British Championship	252	7½/11	
08/90	Lloyds Bank Masters	263	8/10	1=
09/90	Leicester Open		5½/6	1
10/90	Barbican		5½/6	1=
10/90	Hitchin Open		4½/5	1=
11/90	Olympiad		4/8	

BCF GRADES AND FIDE RATINGS

8-10	September 1980	101
9-10	September 1981	128
10-10	September 1982	155
11-10	September 1983	172
12-10	September 1984	192

July	1985	2360 (220)

13-10	September 1985	208

January 1986		2295 (212)
July	1986	2260 (207)

14-10	September 1986	219

January 1987		2360 (220)
July	1987	2360 (220)

15-10	September 1987	227

January 1988		2430 (229)
July	1988	2460 (232)

16-10	September 1988	240

January 1989		2510 (236)
July	1989	2505 (235)

17-10	September 1989	244

January 1990		2555 (244)
July	1990	2590 (249)

18-10	September 1990	246

January 1991		2600 (250)

Highlights of Chess Career

Age

8-0   Celebrated birthday by winning the first tournament he entered, the Cornwall U-10.

8-1   Played first graded game in St Ives-Falmouth match and won his game in 4-2 victory.

8-3   First selection for BCF Junior Squad. Finished third in U-10 event.

8-11 First selection for Cornwall, becoming youngest county player. Drew against J.M.Parker of Devon.

9-2   Became youngest player to win adult competition, winning Falmouth Cup (Cornwall U-125 event).

9-3   Played in Cornwall U-15 and U-18 events simultaneously, winning both, making him youngest winner of county junior championship.

9-9   Finished runner-up in British U-11 at Morecambe.

10-1 Finished joint champion of Plymouth Major event.

10-4 Won BCF Junior Squad U-12.

10-5 Finished runner-up in BCF Junior Squad U-14.

10-6 Led King Charles School to victory in Cornwall Secondary Schools League.

10-7 Led King Charles School to victory in National Primary Schools Team Championships.

10-9 Won British U-11 with record score.

10-11 Filmed "Play Chess" with Bill Hartston for TV.

11-2 Shared County Championship to become youngest player to hold county title.

11-4 Became youngest player to appear in WECU event, scoring 3½/7.

11-7 Led England Primary Schools to victory against Scotland.

11-9 Finished runner-up in British U-14 at Southport.

12-2 Finished third in Plymouth Junior International.

12-2 Won Cornwall Senior title outright.

12-3 Finished third equal in British Lightning event.

12-7 Drew simultaneous game with Gary Kasparov.

12-9 Lost to ex-world champion Spassky in curtain-raiser for Lloyds Bank Masters.

12-9 Defeated first IM opponent, Saeed Ahmed (UAE).

12-11 Completed rating requirements at Chequers Tournament, finishing as runner-up.

13-0 First equal in Torbay Open.

13-4 Joint runner-up in WECU Championship.

13-5 Won BCF Junior Squad U-18 title.

13-7 Became youngest current player to appear on FIDE rating list.

13-7 Won WECU U-18 title.

13-7 Represented England in Glorney Cup in Netherlands.

13-8 Became second youngest player to appear in British Championship, scoring 5/11 in Edinburgh.

13-10 Finished first equal in Paignton event.

13-11 Defeated Jim Plaskett, first GM victim, while winning Hexagon title.

14-1 Drew six-game match in New York against Ilya Gurevich.

14-3 Became youngest player to win WECU title, with record score.

14-4 Won East Devon Open outright.

14-4 Won BCF Junior Squad U-21 title.

14-5 Lost in England Junior Squad simul against Gary Kasparov.

14-7 Played for England in Glorney Cup in Dublin.
14-8 Gained first IM norm, while scoring 7/11 at British Championships in Southampton and finishing sixth equal.
14-9 Won BCF U-21 Quickplay Championship
14-9 Gained second IM norm at Lloyds Bank Masters.
14-10 Successfully defended Hexagon Open title.
15-4 Joint winner of East Devon Open with IM King.
15-5 Retained BCF Junior Squad U-21 title.
15-6 Retained WECU title.
15-7 Runner-up in World U-16 event in Innsbruck.
15-8 Won BCF Junior Squad U-21 Blitz title.
15-8 Scored 7/11 in British Championship at Swansea, finishing sixth equal.
15-9 Finished seventh equal at Lloyds Bank Masters.
15-9 Shared British Isles Open title with four grandmasters – Chandler, Kudrin, Nunn and Rogers.
15-10 Achieved IM all-play-all norm at NatWest Young Masters after thirteen months wait to qualify as youngest IM in world.
16-0 Joint winner of Torbay Open.
16-2 Won Hastings Weekend title.
16-3 Completed hat trick of wins at East Devon Open.
16-4 Finished second equal in Oakham Junior International.
16-4 Completed hat-trick of BCF Junior Squad U-21 titles.
16-7 Scored successive wins against three GMs in British Quickplay.
16-8 Won Charlton Open with six wins.
16-8 Finished fifth equal in British Championship at Blackpool with 7½/11, winning U-21 title.
16-9 Finished first equal in Lloyds Bank Masters, defeating GM Chandler in final round.
16-9 Achieved first GM norm, while sharing first place in NatWest Young Masters.
16-10 Represented England in World Junior in Adelaide.
16-11 Defeated Chandler and Speelman to reach final of James Capel Speed Challenge, losing to Short after four replays in final.
17-0 Finished first equal in Thessaloniki Open, run alongside Olympiad.
17-1 Finished runner-up in Leigh Grand Prix.
17-1 Made debut for Clichy in French League.
17-3 Played in "Generations" Tournament, drawing with ex-world champions Tal and Spassky.
17-3 Won East Devon Open for fourth year.
17-5 Clichy won French League, with Michael scoring 8½/11.
17-5 Won Paris Open outright.
17-7 Achieved second GM norm, while winning Park Hall International outright.
17-7 Played for Truro School in Times British Schools Finals.
17-7 Finished third equal in British Speed Championships.
17-8 Completed GM title requirements at Icklicki Masters, while winning event outright.
17-8 Won British Championship at Plymouth to become youngest ever title holder with 8½/11.
17-10 Finished as runner up in Ostend Open.
17-11 Represented England in World Team Championship at Lucerne. Team won bronze medal.
18-0 Represented England in European Team Championship at Haifa.
18-0 Defeated Hjartarson and Timman to reach final of European Speed Challenge, losing to Speelman in final after replay.
18-1 Won Leigh Grand Prix.
18-1 Played in Hastings Premier, a Category 14 event, the highest ever held in England.
18-4 Represented England in Visa match in Reykjavik and was a member of team that beat USSR for first time ever.

18-6 Finished second equal at British Zonal to qualify for Interzonal.
18-6 Led Truro School to Times British Schools Finals for second successive year.
18-7 Chosen as "Player of the Year".
18-7 Played in World Interzonal in Manila, only just failing to reach Candidates matches.
18-8 Finished fourth equal in British Championship at Eastbourne with 7½/11, remaining unbeaten for second successive year.
18-9 Finished first equal in Lloyds Bank Masters.
19-0 Represented England in Olympiad at Novi Sad.

Index of Players

(numbers refer to games)

Index of Openings

(numbers refer to games)

Pergamon Chess Magazine